True Wealth Defined

The 8 Pillars to Discovering Life's Riches

By BART A. ZANDBERGEN CFP, CDFA

Published by Game Changer Publishing

Printed in the United States

Paperback ISBN: 979-8-90158-390-6

Hardcover ISBN: 979-8-90158-189-6

Digital ISBN: 979-8-90158-190-2

Foreword

When we hear the word "wealth," most of us think of money, possessions, and achievements or accolades. But throughout my life, I've learned that true wealth is built on something deeper and more lasting. And few are truly aligned with me in that understanding more than my friend and financial advisor, Bart Zandbergen.

I met Bart over ten years ago at Lifetime Fitness in Orange County. And what started as casual conversations in the locker room became a meaningful friendship. Over the years, Bart has guided me through major seasons of life and leadership, and he continues to advise me and oversee several of my investment portfolios with integrity and excellence.

But what I admire most about Bart isn't what he does. It's who he is. He's steady, genuine, generous, and a pillar in the community. He's helped many families and leaders, not only financially but personally.

This book is powerful because it reflects the truth Bart lives every day: that wealth is more than just money. His eight pillars of true wealth give us a roadmap to build a life that lasts. They challenge us to measure wealth not only by what we accumulate but by who we become.

I'm honored to call Bart a friend, and I'm grateful for the impact he's made in my life. My prayer is that these pages expand your vision of success and lead you to pursue what truly matters.

Because the richest life is built from the inside out.[1]

— Moses Heredia

[1] Moses Heredia is a current client of The Zandbergen Group. The Zandbergen Group is a DBA of Axxcess Wealth Management, LLC a Registered Investment Advisor with the SEC. He was not compensated for this statement. His experience may not be representative of all clients and is not a guarantee of future performance or success.

Acknowledgments

To my cherished family, dear friends, and mentors who inspire me every day with your unwavering love, support, and encouragement. Your presence fuels my passion and drives me to pursue my dreams with purpose and determination.

To my wonderful and beautiful wife, Tina, my partner for twenty-one amazing years. Your love is the foundation of our family, and your unwavering support has guided me through life's challenges. You have a remarkable ability to see the best in others and uplift them with your kindness. And your inner beauty shines just as brightly as your outer beauty. You inspire me every day with your strength, compassion, and grace. And I'm endlessly grateful for your belief in me and for the countless ways you enrich our lives. Together, we've built a beautiful life, and I look forward to all the adventures still to come.

To my firstborn, Nicole, whose unwavering support and nurturing spirit mirror my own. From the moment you entered this world, I knew you were destined for greatness. Your determination as a single mother is truly remarkable; you balance raising your children with grace and love, always putting their needs first. You possess an innate ability to uplift those around you, and your caring nature has not only shaped your own family but also enriched my life as your father. Thank you for being my confidante, my cheerleader, and a shining example of what it means to be compassionate and driven.

To my sweet son, Christian, your journey has been nothing short of extraordinary. From the mischievous little boy who kept us on our toes, to the devoted father and loving husband you are today, you've grown and evolved into an inspiring man. Your challenges have only made you more empathetic and persistent, and I admire how you've turned those experiences into lessons for your own children. You tirelessly provide for your family, and your dedication to being a present father to your three beautiful children fills my heart with pride. I'm grateful for the bond we share and the joy you bring to our lives.

To my vibrant daughter, Tehani, you're a whirlwind of energy and joy. Your strong-willed nature and brilliant mind light up every room. Watching you embrace life with such enthusiasm is a gift. Your ability to speak two languages fluently at just ten years old is a testament to your intelligence and curiosity. You have a unique spark that inspires those around you to be their best selves, and I'm proud to call you my daughter. Your laughter and adventurous spirit remind me to embrace every moment, and I look forward to witnessing the amazing things you'll accomplish.

To my dear friend and publicist, Paula, thank you for being a constant source of inspiration and encouragement. Your faith in me has pushed me to step outside my comfort zone and embrace new challenges, including writing this book. Over the past ten years, you've been more than just a professional ally. You've become a cherished friend. Your ability to see potential where others may not has motivated me to pursue my dreams wholeheartedly. I appreciate your guidance, laughter, and unwavering support, and I'm excited to see what the future holds for both of us.

To my friend and mentor, Moses Heredia, author of *Fields to Fortune*. You're an example of whom I aspire to be. Your wisdom, integrity, and dedication to your craft motivate me to strive for excellence. Thank you for your guidance and for showing me the true meaning of success.

To my incredible Zandbergen Group Team: Sandi, Danielle, Wyatt, and Jon. Without your hard work, dedication, and support, I couldn't perform to the best of my abilities. You're the backbone of our success, and I'm grateful for the endless contributions you make for our clients and for me. Infinite thanks for all that you do!

To my valued clients, thank you for the years of trust and confidence you've placed in me and my team. Your belief in our abilities motivates us to deliver our best. I'm honored to partner with you on your journeys and to be a part of your true wealth success stories.

To God, I give thanks and praise for all the blessings you've bestowed upon me. Your guidance and grace have been my constant companions, and I'm grateful for the opportunities and challenges that have shaped my life. Thank you for your unwavering presence and for the strength to pursue my dreams.

***Disclosures:** This book is provided for informational and educational purposes only and should not be construed as investment, legal, or tax advice. The views expressed are the author's personal opinions and are not intended as recommendations to buy or sell any security or implement any investment strategy. The Zandbergen Group is a DBA of Axxcess Wealth Management, LLC a Registered Investment Advisor with the SEC.

Contents

What If Wealth Wasn't Just About Money?

"Better what the eye sees than the roving of the appetite.
This too is meaningless..."
Ecclesiastes 6:9

What if most of us have built entire lives around a definition of wealth that was never designed to satisfy *us*?

Our modern-day culture glorifies the concept of the "hustle." More is always better: a bigger house, a newer car, a higher net worth, a larger following. The world teaches us to chase milestones that glitter but rarely satisfy for longer than a few minutes; the effect fading once it's no longer new and shiny. And social media fuels the illusion that everyone else seems to be making it, so if you're not "keeping up," you must be doing something wrong.

But what happens when you *do* hit the goals? What happens when you get the job title, the benefits package, and the seven-figure bank account... and something still feels off?

We misunderstand wealth because the industries that claim to teach about it often frame it through a narrow perspective. Early in my career, I sat in rooms where success was only measured by quarterly numbers, sales rankings, production awards, and page-long financial statements. If the charts pointed up, your life should feel complete. Or at least, that's the message we're taught, right? The worlds of business, technology, and finance reward measurable results, so they've trained us to equate progress with accumulation. The trouble is, most of what brings meaning in life isn't actually measurable. Or rather, not measurable in the ways we track business statistics.

Through my career in financial advising, I've met people with impressive balance sheets who felt empty, anxious, or disconnected from their life's work and struggled with finding passion or lasting joy. On the other hand, I've also met people with modest means who had strong relationships, supportive communities, and steady lives that felt whole and flooded with self-driven passion. But does that mean that wealth and joy aren't connected? Or even, are at odds with one another? Not inherently, and as we continue, we'll explore why that is. For now, consider that the point isn't about how much money someone has but about what's supporting their lives outside of their finances.

Many people chase financial milestones because they believe money alone will eventually deliver the peace, confidence, or fulfillment they can't seem to find within themselves. But money doesn't create those qualities. It only magnifies what already exists, so when the foundation is weak, more money intensifies the cracks. But when the foundation is strong, money becomes a tool rather than a master.

My parents were immigrants, and life in our home was tough financially, emotionally, and psychologically. Abuse and bullying were constants, and I learned early on that nothing was going to be handed to me. I had to earn everything. So, I did what a lot of people do when they come from instability: I chased stability. I worked hard. I got educated. I found ways to climb every ladder I could find. I kept moving and hustling, doing the same things the world teaches us will lead to a successful and fulfilled life. And it worked—to a point.

Stability meant different things to me at different ages. As a kid, stability meant a quiet morning or a day without conflict and knowing what version of home I was walking into after school. It meant hoping the bullying would stay outside instead of following me through the front door, or that the bully's family would suddenly move to another district. Back then, stability felt like a luxury because it was so rare, and that's not even taking into account the mental and emotional rockiness that came with the territory of merely growing up.

As a teenager, stability became about control. I wanted control over my weight, my grades, and my future. I studied hard because school gave me a kind of structure that life at home didn't. And exercise became another kind of structure. Running and surfing gave me a sense of progress no one could take away, and gave me the strength and health to be able to engage with the world and people around me.

Stability changed from being about emotional safety to becoming a personal discipline.

As a young adult, stability meant financial security. I learned new skills and grabbed every opportunity that crossed my path, believing that financial success would fix everything I lacked growing up. I thought a steady paycheck, a reliable car, a small home, and a young marriage would solve the rest. And that belief pushed me through college, career changes, and long nights of work. But it also pushed me into an indescribable emotional strain as I tried to hold it all together. I was driven by a simple idea that if I earned enough, life would finally feel safe, regardless of how unsafe the rest of the elements at play were.

Later, as an adult deep in my career, I became stronger because of personal struggles (which we'll talk more about later), and the idea of stability changed again, but now, it was all about *balance*. Stability meant waking up without dread and going to sleep without regret. It meant relationships that felt steady because they *were* steady, a peaceful home full of love, joy, and passion, and a body and mind that could support the life I wanted. Stability was no longer a metric but a state of being.

I went from a business degree to computer programming to sales before eventually becoming a financial advisor. And along the way, I earned a solid income and a respectable reputation, in addition to all the outward signs of success. I earned the perception of someone who'd "made it." But there were days I felt like I was living someone else's dream, and sometimes, my own nightmare. For a while, I chased a version of wealth that society sold to me, but it didn't match the life I wanted to be living. So, I began to ask myself, *what is wealth, really?*

That question led me on a path through coaching programs, personal breakthroughs, spiritual development, relationship challenges, and *a lot* of self-reflection. And over time, I began to see patterns in my own life, in my clients' lives, and in the lives of those I admired most. It wasn't big bank accounts or an extensive list of accomplishments that allowed someone to be truly "rich." In fact. financial status had nothing to do with it. Regardless of what end of the spectrum someone fell into, the people who had the "riches" lives were the ones who had harmony, purpose, peace, and fulfillment that stemmed from *within themselves.*

That's when the concept of True Wealth began.

True Wealth is a way of living, a holistic alignment of values, relationships, habits, and service. And I started defining what that looked like for me. I began creating a framework that could be both aspirational and practical; something I could live by, and something I could share. And over the years, this framework has become the foundation of how I live, advise, mentor, and speak.

And now, it's the foundation of this book.

Although money *is* part of this story, this book isn't a financial guide. I've spent decades helping people manage investments, retirement strategies, insurance decisions, and long-term planning. And those tools are valuable, but they don't tell someone how to build a truly meaningful life. Finance deals with numbers, but life planning deals with people. Yet many clients came into my office hoping better financial organization would fix their stress or strained relationships. They believed more money would eventually create the purpose they were missing, but it rarely worked that way.

So, if you opened this book looking for stock tips, tax strategies, or retirement formulas, you won't find them here. Our society is already saturated with investment advice from podcasts, YouTube channels, TikTok "gurus," and a thousand different voices telling us how to make, save, invest, or grow our money. What we don't have enough of is guidance on how to *build a life*.

Money *is* one of the eight pillars of True Wealth, but it's the last one for a reason. Money without health is useless. Money without relationships is lonely. Money without faith, purpose, or self-acceptance becomes a burden.

So instead, think of this book as a conversation about the parts of your life that influence your happiness more than your bank statements, and about the things that can't be measured but always matter. Finance will be a topic we cover, but it shows up as the tool it's always been meant to be instead of the driving force of our experiences.

This book focuses on everything that money can't buy but still influences how we use it. There are elements in our lives which shape the way money functions for each of us, on a personal and professional level. Without those pieces, financial planning becomes a technical exercise without the emotional stability to support it. But with those pieces in place, financial decisions become clearer and more grounded. This is a conversation about building a life where money supports us as whole people instead of overshadowing who we are and what we dream of.

You'll be introduced to the eight pillars that make up what I call True Wealth:

1. Health
2. Family & Friends
3. Faith
4. Service to Others
5. Legacy
6. Peace
7. The Invisibles
8. Finance

As I said, finance *is* one of the pillars, but it's the final one, and we'll get more into the why as we go.

But first, we'll begin with Health, because without physical, mental, and emotional well-being, every other area of life suffers. I'll tell you about my transition from being an overweight, bullied kid to someone who wakes up at 3:30 a.m. to work out, motivated by raw gratitude. We'll talk about what it means to take care of the one body and mind you've got, both for yourself and for the people who count on you.

Then we'll move into Family & Friends. Real wealth is in the moments and the people that make life decadent. I'll share what I've learned about developing deep relationships, surviving divorce, parenting at different life stages, and finding connection in a disconnected world.

Faith comes next. Stay with me here, because whatever your beliefs, we all need something bigger than ourselves to anchor us, regardless of what we call it or where we believe it comes from. And for me, my Faith in God has been a steadying force, especially in the toughest seasons. I'll describe how belief, prayer, and purpose have shaped my experiences, and why faith often shows up again and again in the lives of the world's longest-living, most fulfilled people.

Service to Others is a pillar that humbles. Giving is about so much more than writing checks. It's about living in a way that leaves the world better than you found it. From philanthropy to mentorship, and team building to community engagement, we'll dig into how generosity is one of the most powerful currencies.

From there, we'll consider Legacy. Many people confuse legacy as being about what we leave behind, but it's actually about what we build while we're here and if it can outlive us once we're no longer around to maintain it. We'll talk about how to think long-term, how to align your life with your values, and how to make sure the best parts of yourself outlive you (and it has nothing to do with awards).

The Peace pillar is the one I wrestle with the most. Monkey brain, anxiety, the inability to slow down and be present—I know the struggle. But I've also discovered practices and mindsets that help create space for stillness. Peace of mind and peace with oneself are necessary in finding true fulfillment in life.

This next one is tricky. The Invisibles are moments that don't make it into spreadsheets or Instagram posts, but they make all the difference. A sincere "I love you" from your child, witnessing the sunset with someone you care about, a deep breath on a hard day; these are the small moments that make up a big life which we often take for granted when our heads are stuck in hustle culture.

Then, finally, we'll talk about Finance, though not in the way you might expect, but in a way that integrates everything else. I'll share what I've learned from decades in the industry, the wisdom I wish I'd had at twenty, thirty, or even forty. And we'll talk about managing money with purpose, and how to let money serve your life instead of running it.

You don't have to be in crisis to need a change. You don't have to hit rock bottom to ask better questions. You don't have to wait for something to break before you start building something stronger. You can be successful, stable, and surrounded by good things, and still feel like there's something missing. And if any of this sounds familiar to you, I'm glad you're here.

This book is for anyone who senses a gap between how life looks and how life feels. It's for people who have reached certain milestones and wondered why the satisfaction didn't last. It's for anyone entering a new season, where priorities change and old habits no longer fit. It's for people recovering from hardship or rising from a transition, trying to rebuild with more understanding than before. It's for high achievers who fear slowing down, caregivers who put themselves last, and quiet strivers who want their efforts to mean something.

Whether you're building the early shape of your life, reevaluating the middle of it, or reflecting on what you'll leave behind, the questions remain the same. What matters? What sustains you? What aligns with your values? What brings lasting peace? True Wealth invites you to examine your life through those perspectives and decide what you want the next chapter of your life to *feel* like, not just look like.

I don't have all the answers. In fact, I'd be a fool if I tried to make such a bold statement. But I do have a life that feels full. And I got here by accepting that life comes with challenges, but it's what we do with the realities of life that matter.

It's hard to be married.

It's hard to be divorced.

It's hard to be fit and healthy.

It's hard to be sick and unhealthy.

Pick your hard. Then build your wealth.

Every morning in Africa, the sun rises. Every morning in Africa, a gazelle wakes up. It knows it must outrun the fastest lion, or it'll be killed. Every morning in Africa, a lion wakes up. It knows it must outrun the slowest gazelle, or it'll starve. Which means, whether you're a lion or a gazelle, when the sun comes up, you better be running. You just need to determine what you're running toward.

You need to pick your hard and push through it.

Redefining Wealth: A Life of Meaning

"A good person leaves an inheritance for their children's children..."
Proverbs 13:22

Let's start with an exercise. Pick a number between one and ten. It can be any number within that range. Now, multiply it by nine. If you have a double digit, add the two numbers together. Still have a double digit? Add them together again. Then, subtract five.

Next, map the result to a letter of the alphabet (A=1, B=2, etc.). Do you have it? Now, using that letter, think of a country that starts with that letter. Then, think of the letter that comes next in the alphabet from the one you just used (toward Z; A > B, B > C, etc.). Now, think of an animal that starts with that new letter. And finally, think of the color of that animal.

What did you write down? If you came up with a gray elephant in Denmark, it's not magic, nor is it a coincidence. It's because we're all conditioned to think similarly. What that little exercise shows is conditioning. Most of us make the same choices because we all travel the same mental paths. That's how culture works. Advertising repeats a message, schools reward a certain kind of achievement, industries publish leaderboards that celebrate outputs but rarely ask what those outputs cost. And over time, our minds stop asking if the measurements are right. We only ask how to score higher. The same thing happens with wealth. So, if the only chart we see is net worth, we let it decide how we feel about our lives.

But what if we've been conditioned to think about wealth incorrectly in the process?

Back in the mid-80s and early 90s, I was laser-focused on building my career. I jumped into computer programming at Rockwell International right after school, and only a year later, I moved on to Ford Aerospace. But I didn't love big corporate America. I had a goal to eventually get into computer sales instead, but to do that, I had to take a sales support position. Which is what I did when I left Ford after two years to work at Diebold, a multinational financial and retail technology company at the forefront of point-of-sale machines and ATMs. I had to start from the bottom rungs as a support sales associate, but I got my foot in the door, which helped me later get into a sales position with ABBA Computer Systems.

I learned how to cold call at ABBA and started meeting with company representatives in person. I figured out how to make the hustle and grind work for me. I closed. I delivered. Rinse and repeat. And it paid off. I was successful, at least by traditional standards. I met all my financial goals by the age of thirty. I had a thriving client base and all the trappings of someone who'd "won the game." I'd done everything I was "supposed to" do. But I didn't feel like I'd actually gained anything *meaningful.*

My health was an afterthought. My relationships were suffering. And my mind was always chasing. Or rather, *escaping.* Work had become an escape from the challenges in my personal life with my then-wife, but aside from the money and the freedom from what was happening at home, what else did my career really provide for me and my children?

It was during this time that I realized I wanted more from life and my career. I wanted to change lives. I'd recently met with my financial advisor, and when discussing this epiphany with him, he said, "You know, what I do here is changing lives. You might consider this as a career." So, like most big decisions in my life, I sat on that thought for several months. Until one night, about 2:00 a.m., I sat up and, with complete certainty, said to myself, "I'm going to do this."

The following year was challenging. I worked my sales job during the day and took classes and passed exams for the needed licensing at night. I even helped my new advisory firm by making seminar follow-up calls. Until the day came when I was able to leave my job and become a full-time financial advisor instead. Keep in mind, I left a six-figure job with impressive benefits to become self-employed, starting from $0. Although not immediately, and not without thought. Still, it was a risk, but even more so, it was a huge change from the lifestyle I'd grown accustomed to during that in-between period.

My true-wealth "ah-ha" came about ten years into my career as a financial advisor, when I encountered the initial concept through a training program called Carson Coaching (which became the seed that eventually developed into the True Wealth pillars). It sounded like a nice idea from the beginning, a soft counterpoint to hard finance. But the more I sat with it, the more layered the concept became. And the more I looked at the lives of my clients, colleagues, friends, and mentors, the more I saw the same pattern: success without fulfillment is just a prettier kind of failure.

Real "wealth" isn't measured in what we can count. It's measured in what *counts most*. And the more I reflected on that, the more I realized how deeply systemic our misunderstanding of wealth is. We've all been fed the same story since childhood that the ultimate goal is to accumulate—hoard, even. To gain more money to buy more stuff. To acquire more status or followers or influence. We're trained to believe that success equals *more* and that our value is tied to our output. But when we chase that story to its end, we typically find burnout instead of accomplishment.

We see it everywhere: lottery winners who end up bankrupt within five years because they weren't equipped to handle sudden financial inflation; celebrities who have fame, fortune, and admiration, yet battle addiction, depression, and isolation; executives with multimillion-dollar salaries who have heart attacks in their fifties and don't recognize their own kids.

Money isn't inherently bad. It's just a concept we've created to manage the collection and use of our resources. But when it becomes the sole measure of our success, it warps everything else. Families fracture over inheritance disputes, and marriages slowly erode under the pressure of constant striving. And professionals who look impeccable on LinkedIn may be secretly crumbling behind the scenes. We're a society of exhausted achievers.

Of course, most people don't wake up one morning and say, "I'm going to lose myself in achievement." It happens slowly and usually without us noticing it. We start by setting one goal. Perhaps to earn more, build more, or become more. And for a while, the path feels exciting. Every milestone we hit gives us a dopamine hit, a quick shot of validation that makes the next goal feel even more urgent. But the chase has a side effect. While we're running toward something, we often run past what matters.

Nobody teaches us how to detect when ambition has crossed into addiction. Nobody teaches us how to recognize when striving turns into escaping. We don't notice the fatigue at first, or the resentment. or the emotional distance. We just keep going because everything around us rewards speed instead of intentionality.

There's a simple way to think about misplaced focus. You can't find Mr. Right when you're spending time with Mr. Wrong. Or, framed another way, you won't find a better job if all your energy goes into a role you don't care about. You'll miss out on joy when your mind stays locked on negativity. What we focus on becomes the only thing we're about the recognize around us, for better or worse.

That's why redefining wealth matters. If you don't define wealth for yourself, the world will define it for you. And the world's definition is relentless and empty.

Real wealth begins when you stop running long enough to ask, "Where am I going, and why?" Because if you don't know the answer, the chase owns you. And that's never where freedom lives.

Every field invents its scoreboard. Business has revenue, followers, and titles. Finance has assets and returns. And these metrics are useful, but they're not *neutral.* They teach us to chase what they measure. And if we're not careful, we wake up fluent in charts and illiterate in our own lives. The numbers rise, and so does the distance between how we live and what we value.

Granted, just like money, "more" isn't inherently bad either, as it can bring good things into our lives, such as more security and freedom. But everything in life comes with consequences, even good things. More responsibility and options put us in a position to contend with more pressure, more distraction, and become more at risk of detachment from what really matters.

There's a cost to chasing the wrong definition of wealth. And that cost often shows up as broken relationships, neglected health, emotional numbness, spiritual emptiness, and an aching sense of disconnection from purpose. We're told to accumulate, but we aren't taught to *align*. We're told to build empires, but we're not shown how to *build lives.*

But that's where True Wealth comes in.

The more I really sat with the concept, the more I saw the consequences of a narrow definition of wealth. Both in my own life and in the lives of others. Wealth isn't the same thing as money, despite how deeply we've convinced ourselves otherwise. Money is merely a piece of it. But wealth—real, meaningful, soul-deep wealth—is something else entirely.

It's the ability to wake up with energy and purpose. To spend time with the people we love without checking our phones every five minutes. To live in alignment with our values. To serve something bigger than ourselves. To breathe deeply, love generously, and sleep peacefully. And those aren't things we can put on a spreadsheet and submit to the tax office. They're something we build with intention.

Meaning, if your life looks great on paper but feels empty in practice, it's time to reconsider what you're measuring. Ask yourself:

- What *are* you measuring?
- Who taught you that those metrics mattered more than other metrics?
- And what might your life look like if you started measuring differently?

As I started piecing together what real wealth looked like, the patterns emerged. The people who seemed deeply fulfilled, grounded, and at peace were successful in how they *lived*, not just within their careers. And it wasn't one thing holding everything up. It was a collection of values and habits, each distinct but interconnected, which have become the eight pillars of True Wealth. When one pillar wobbles, the others absorb the load. When several crack, life feels thin, even when money is strong. And that pattern holds so consistently, it became the framework for this book.

The Eight Pillars of True Wealth

Health: The Foundation

You can't enjoy wealth if you don't have the energy to live.

As I touched on, when I was younger, I didn't take health seriously. I was the overweight kid. I was bullied, sluggish, and stuck in my head. But later, I reclaimed that part of my life. And today, I get up at 3:30 a.m. to train. It has less to do with *looking* a certain way, though. I have no explicit plans to impress anyone except myself. But I want to respect myself and respect the body I've been given to experience the wonders of the world with and through. I do it because health is the foundation of everything we do. And without it, I can't lead, serve, or love well. And I've seen the difference in my clients, too. Those who prioritize their health (not obsessively but intentionally) have more stamina, more confidence, and experience more joy.

Wealth starts with vitality.

Family & Friends: Your Real Net Worth

True wealth is measured in moments. I've worked with many clients who built significant financial success only to realize they'd drifted from the people they loved most. I've also watched families come back together when priorities changed.

Family and close friendships give life texture. They ground and challenge us. They remind us of who we are and who we're becoming. If your calendar doesn't reflect time with the people who matter, your "net worth" is dropping.

Faith: The Anchor and Shield in Every Storm

I've been burned by life enough times to know I can't do this life alone.

My Faith in God has been a constant for me, even when I couldn't articulate it. It's what steadies me when logic fails. For some, it's God. For others, it's spirituality, philosophy, or universal values. But regardless of the form, faith gives us context. It helps us see beyond the immediate and strengthens our perseverance. And it reminds us that we're not the center of the universe, nor are we alone.

Service to Others: The Currency of Purpose

Serving others is one of the most undervalued expressions of wealth.

Early in my life, I gave because I felt I was "supposed to." Now, I give because I *get* to. Whether it's mentoring a young professional, volunteering, or making space for others to improve, service expands us. It takes us beyond self-interest and into social impact.

Many of my clients find that their most joyful moments come when they're helping someone else rise.

Legacy: What Money Can't Buy and Death Can't Take Away

When people hear "legacy," they think of wills, trusts, or charitable foundations. And that's part of it, but a legacy is also how we treat our teams, how we raise our kids, and how we show up when no one's watching.

Consider what story your life tells when you're gone. If you don't like the answer, it's never too late to edit the script.

Peace: The Wealth of a Quiet Mind

Peace isn't about being calm all the time but living in a way that quiets the internal and external chaos. Many of us struggle with anxiety, especially when we overextended. But when we create space for silence, whether through prayer, walks, journaling, or simply breathing, we return to our center.

My clients who've achieved peace often describe it as the most valuable shift in their lives. It changes how we make decisions, how we love, and how we lead.

The Invisibles: The Moments You Can't Measure

This pillar is the hardest to describe, but the easiest to feel. It's the quiet morning with your child, the unexpected laugh with your spouse, and the deep exhale after a meaningful conversation, among others. We can't "obtain" these things. They already exist around us each day. But we can start experiencing them first-hand by learning how to notice and appreciate them, instead of allowing them to pass us by passively. And, in tandem with the other elements, we can develop more opportunities for these moments to take place. They're experiences you can't frame and hang on the walls, but which are the glue of a meaningful life.

When we chase only what we can quantify, we miss what makes us human.

Finance: The Tool, Not the Goal

Yes, money matters. Yes, you need to manage it wisely. But money exists to serve your values, not the other way around. In my career, I've seen money ruin good people, and I've seen good people do extraordinary things with very little. It all comes down to what you do with what you have, regardless of how "much" you have.

When finance *supports* the other pillars, it creates freedom. When it replaces them, it creates a trap.

Each of these eight pillars can stand on their own. But together, they build a life that's not just rich but truly wealthy.

Throughout the coming chapters, I'll be sharing stories from my own life, interactions with other people, and moments that reshaped how I think about wealth. And every chapter will include questions and tools to help you define and align your life around what matters most, too.

The goal is to come out of this book with the skills to:

- Build routines that support your physical and emotional health
- Strengthen relationships that matter
- Reconnect with your sense of faith or deeper purpose
- Contribute meaningfully to others
- Create a legacy you're proud of
- Find peace in a chaotic world
- Celebrate small, invisible moments
- Use money as a resource instead of a scorecard.

But to create and maintain these awarenesses and skills, we need to start one step at a time and build one on top of the other. And we need to be honest with ourselves about where we've been falling short. So, as we move forward, I invite you to think about this question:

What would your life look like if you didn't only measure success by what you owned but also by what you experienced, how you served, and how you loved?

But first, let's pause for a moment. You've made it through a lot already. You've been introduced to what it could be. And maybe, just maybe, you're starting to feel a little uncomfortable. But if that's the case, *good*. That means we're getting somewhere. We all need to reflect and engage with ourselves to redesign our habits to align with our values.

You're the architect of your own life, but maybe you've been using someone else's blueprint. Or maybe you've been renovating without really looking at the foundation. Or perhaps you've built something solid but want to add more meaning, connection, and joy. Wherever you are, you can start now.

True Wealth can only be achieved through design. And design requires intention. It requires choosing what matters, repeatedly, even when it's inconvenient. And sometimes, *especially* when it's inconvenient. It means saying no to things that look impressive but feel empty. It means setting boundaries around our time, energy, and attention, and sticking to those boundaries. It's simple in concept but not easy in execution, at least not at the beginning. But the more comfortable we can become with looking at our lives through the perspective of the eight pillars and learning how to make changes that realign them, the more genuinely fulfilling our lives become.

I've seen marriages revived because someone decided to be present again. I've watched executives finally take care of their bodies and regain energy they hadn't had in years. I've seen people reconnect with their faith and discover a kind of peace they never thought possible. These are human transformations. They're messy, imperfect, and sometimes consuming and energy-draining steps forward that take awareness and courage. And a deep, authentic desire to actually *do something* with the lives we have instead of allowing life to *do things to us*.

You don't have to overhaul your life this week. That would be impossible. And nothing is sustainable if we try to power-level through it. But you do have to start paying attention. What's draining you? What's nourishing you? What story are you telling with your habits, your relationships, and even your calendar?

There's a version of your life that feels more whole and freer. You may not see it yet, but you can perhaps sense it. That quiet nudge that says, "You were made for more than this corporate treadmill." And on your way to becoming that version of yourself, you'll face internal resistance. You'll bump up against old habits, external expectations, and your own inner critic. You'll be tempted to go back to what's easy. And that's not even considering the resistance you might face from other people. But "easy" isn't the goal.

So, what do you do next?

You start small. You take one pillar at a time and ask yourself how you could give it more care. Maybe it's your health. Maybe your relationships. Maybe you need to finally sit still long enough to hear your own thoughts again. There's no perfect place to start. But you *need* to start. And as you go, remember that you're not racing anyone.

You're not behind. You're not broken. You're building, one moment and one decision at a time.

But *which* pillar should you start with? Well, that's technically up to you. All the pillars tie into one another and are supposed to be used all together. That said, optimally, it's best to save the pillar of money for last. Because putting that pillar first is precisely why many of us end up in the position where we don't feel truly fulfilled. So for now, set it aside and focus on the other elements of True Wealth first.

There's no perfect place to start, but there is a practical one. Which is why I recommend starting with the pillar of health. Because without taking care of our bodies, we can't put in the effort and energy for the rest of the pillars. So start where every other pillar depends; start with the body you live in.

Health isn't the whole of True Wealth, but it's the foundation that everything stands on.

Health: The Foundation

"Your body is a temple of the Holy Spirit... therefore honor God with your body."
1 Corinthians 6:19–20

Health and fitness influencers across the internet display their hard-earned abs and film "What I Eat in-a Day" videos of their favorite freshly pressed green juice recipes. Including myself, because I enjoy sharing what the human body is capable of and encouraging others to make health and wellness decisions for themselves.

But I didn't start out there. Specifically, my relationship with health started on the complete opposite end of the spectrum. I was an overweight preteen and teenager (which wasn't helped by my mother's bad modeling of a cigarette in the morning and a box of donuts or cheap cereal for breakfast). Picture a chubby, awkward middle school kid trying to survive each day while dodging insults, jokes, and looks that told me I didn't belong. I'd walk the hallway and feel emotionally invisible, or worse, like the punchline everyone was waiting to use. I joined the Boy Scouts at one point, but even there, I was bullied.

Bart (on left) pictured with Grandmother Oma, and his siblings, Tim and Trudy.

There's a loneliness to that kind of experience. And it burrows deep. I started to believe I wasn't enough: wasn't strong enough, fast enough, good-looking enough. And that maybe I never would be. I withdrew. I overate. And ultimately, I felt stuck in my own body.

One day, I rode my bike to my hometown theater. The movie "Rocky" was playing. I had my soda and popcorn, and I was utterly inspired. There was a guy who was disrespected and made fun of, yet whom I completely identified with. The movie lit something within me, and I said to myself, "I'm going to rewrite my story."

So, I started running. I started with one neighborhood block the first day, two the second, and so on. And from there, I gained a love for swimming and surfing, and I used those sports to help me trim down even more. I also read a book called *Sugar Blues* by William Dufty, which educated me about how bad sugar is for the body. And before I graduated high school, I went from being the butt of the jokes to getting attention from and "stealing girls" from the same athletes who'd picked on me in the years before, just because I was becoming fit. The summer between ninth and tenth grade, I lost 30 lbs, grew three inches, and my hair grew longer and turned blond from the ocean while surfing. And by the time I reached college, I'd started to lift weights too.

Bart, age 17

Health saved me before wealth had a chance to. It gave me confidence and offered the early signs that I could change my life through intentional action, not just hope. And that belief became the bedrock for everything else I would build later.

The thing is, though, unless I tell people about my fitness journey, it's easy to assume that my workout regimen, my dietary routine, my energy, and my discipline had always been this way. But my current habits were born from pain, necessity, and choice, not convenience.

But if it had all come from convenience, what would that have really done for me? You can buy a trainer, but you can't buy the discipline to actually follow through. You can sign up for the fanciest gym in town, but if you don't show up consistently and put in the effort, nothing changes. Health isn't about access. It's about ownership and accountability. And that's where a lot of people get stuck.

To make health sustainable during busy seasons, I use baselines and minimums. A baseline is the normal routine, and a minimum is the smallest meaningful action on hard days. Meaning, if the baseline is a full workout, the minimum might be a twenty-minute walk and a few sets of push-ups. Or if the baseline is a home-cooked dinner, the minimum might be a simple protein shake, a piece of fruit, and water. Minimums keep momentum alive even when we have a rough day, which matters more than some unattainable concept of perfection.

So why have we been caught in that trap? Because we've been conditioned to think health is about shortcuts. Magic pills, juice cleanses, supplements with more syllables than nutrients—we're sold the idea that if we just buy the "right thing," we'll look and feel the part. Just look at Kim Kardashian, who promoted appetite-suppressing lollipops to her millions of followers back in 2018. But real health doesn't come in a bottle or from a surgeon's table. It comes from boring, unsexy, consistent choices, and actually following through.

It's drinking water instead of soda. It's walking after dinner instead of scrolling on your phone. It's cooking your own meals, getting decent sleep, stretching, sweating, breathing. And most of all, it's showing up, even when you don't feel like it. And trust me, there will be many days when you just don't feel like it.

Health Myths We've Been Fed

- Myth #1: *Supplements equal health.* No. Supplements are called that because they supplement an already healthy lifestyle. They don't replace movement, rest, or real food.
- Myth #2: *An expensive gym means effort.* No. Some of the healthiest people I know work out in their garages or use bodyweight routines in their living rooms.
- Myth #3: *There's a shortcut to lasting change.* Sorry, but also no. There are faster ways to lose weight or gain muscle temporarily, but none of them beat sustainability.

Health isn't a six-week TikTok challenge. It's a lifetime commitment.

I've worked with incredibly successful clients who ignored their health for years. They built empires on broken bodies and stressed-out minds. And when it finally caught up with them, they realized what I discovered through reflecting back on "Rocky" as I grew older: that you can't enjoy your wealth if your body and mind can't carry you.

You don't need to become a bodybuilder. You don't need to run marathons. But you need to move. You need to fuel your body. You need to sleep, hydrate, recover, and respect the incredible flesh machine you've been given. Your body is your first home. And it's the asset that supports every other part of your life.

Let's start with a lie that most of us have swallowed at one point or another: money guarantees health.

After all, wealthy people have access to the best doctors, the most exclusive gyms, and personal chefs, so we assume they must be healthy. But access doesn't equal commitment, and money can't sweat for you. It can't put the fork down. It can't get you out of bed when it's dark and cold and your pillow feels like a slice of heaven. Some of the wealthiest individuals are physically depleted, mentally fried, and emotionally checked out because they thought their financial success would carry over into their health, but you can't outsource being fit and healthy. And health doesn't care how much you earn. It only cares about how much you move.

But movement doesn't have to mean lifting weights or joining a gym to use fancy equipment. It can mean taking the stairs to the office instead of riding the elevator. Or parking farther away from the coffee shop and walking. If you spend a lot of time at a desk, it can mean getting a standing desk and a walking pad, so you can keep active while you work. Or it can mean doing a few jumping jacks between tasks. There are ways, in each of our lives, for us to integrate just a little more movement without disrupting our daily routines.

Micro-movements change how a day feels. Ten air squats while coffee brews. A five-minute walk after lunch. Hip openers while a call is on mute. Calf raises while brushing your teeth. None of these replace training, but they ensure the body doesn't live at zero between workouts.

For me, what works best is waking up at 3:30 a.m. because that's when I get *me* back. Before the emails and client calls, I move my body and clear my head to anchor my day. It's the act of saying, every day, that my health matters enough to fight for it, and proving it by following through.

Granted, my morning routine might sound extreme, but it's what works *for me.* And over the years, my training has changed. I lift with more attention to form. I warm up longer. I treat recovery as part of the session instead of an afterthought. If an injury flares up, I do what I can without losing the habit of showing up. A lot of people give up on their health and wellness goals because they believe that they can't make adjustments that work for them, but that's the only way to protect the habit. And now, my workout routine and lifestyle habits are what keep me grounded.

I lift weights. I do cardio. I stretch. I drink water first thing in the morning. I journal and pray. I stay off my phone until I've *earned* access to the world again. All in the name of my physical and mental wellness.

And the night before matters too. Sleep is a non-negotiable. No late-night scrolling. No eating two hours before bed. No crashing on the couch and waking up groggy at 2:00 a.m. My evening routine is just as intentional as my morning routine because without proper recovery, I won't have the energy to sustain me through the next day.

What I eat now is also light-years away from where I started. As mentioned, my mother's idea of breakfast when I was growing up was donuts or a box of sugary cereal. So, as you can imagine, my relationship with food was "easy." My taste buds were on a permanent sugar high, and I didn't think twice about what I was putting into my body.

That doesn't mean my meals today are joyless. I still occasionally eat pizza and allow myself to eat fun things in moderation. But the difference is, I have a baseline, a default mode that keeps me aligned with who I want to be, helping me keep my meals intentionally balanced. I eat to perform, to think clearly, and to recover well. I live on self-developed discipline instead of sugar, because I've seen what happens when I allow my health to slip.

My Personal Meal Plan

A structured approach to food became one of the most reliable tools in supporting my long-term health. It's given each day consistency and helped remove unnecessary decisions.

Below is a sample of the meal plan used most often in my daily life. It grew out of years of trial, reflection, and adjustments, and helped stabilize my energy, support training, and keep nutrition simple during demanding seasons. While this is my plan, it's meant only as an example for you. It's not a standard to meet or a prescription to follow. Every person has different needs, preferences, restrictions, and rhythms. The goal isn't to copy these meals but to see how structure can make healthy choices easier. I encourage adapting, modifying, or building your own routine based on what supports your lifestyle. The real value comes from consistency, awareness, and alignment with personal goals, not from following any single menu.

3:45 a.m.	**Pre-Workout Shake**	
		2 scoops vanilla Grass-Fed Whey Protein Isolate 1 scoop greens powder 1 scoop SuperHMO Prebiotic Mix 1 scoop Organic Red Polyphenols Fruit Powder 1 scoop Organic Apple Peel Powder 5 mgs Creatine powder 5 mgs BCAA powder 5 mgs Nitric oxide powder 12 oz Alkaline water

7:30 a.m.	**Post-Workout Shake**	
		2 scoops Momentum Grass-Fed Meal Replacement

		1 scoop mocha Grass-Fed Whey Protein Isolate 1 scoop collagen 5 mgs ARMRA powder 5 mgs BCAA powder 12 oz Alkaline water
10:00 a.m.	**Snack**	
		6 hard-boiled eggs (3 yolks) 1 apple
12:30 p.m.	**Lunch**	
		1.5 cups rice or sweet potatoes 8 oz protein (ground beef, bison, elk, or chicken)
3:00 p.m.	**Snack**	
		Jerky or yogurt w/berries and grain-free granola
6:00 p.m.	**Dinner**	
	Bart Salad	Giant bowl of romaine or mixed greens Fermented carrots Fermented beets 8 oz protein (ground beef, bison, elk, or chicken) Sourdough croutons

Primal Avocado Oil Dressing

Or…

Bart Primavera

Sauteed onions, asparagus, mushrooms
Sauteed cauliflower rice
8 oz protein (ground beef, bison, elk, or chicken)
Organic pasta sauce
Raw parmesan cheese

My Personal Workout Plan

Movement has been one of the most dependable anchors in my life. It supported me during stressful seasons, kept my energy steady, and reminded me each day that health is built through action, not merely through good intention. My workout routine grew over decades of trial and error, including setbacks and slow improvements. Over the last two decades, I've had two torn rotator surgeries, one ruptured quad tendon surgery, and I deal with multiple herniated discs in my lower back. I had to change and adapt it to accommodate my injuries and goals over the years. But it reflects the same principles found throughout this chapter: that health comes from small, repeatable choices made long before the results show up. And developing and expanding the capacity for discipline and lasting habits translates outside of physical wellness as well.

The plan below is my personal structure as of 2026. But just like with my meal plan, it's not meant to be universal. Everybody has different needs, limitations, and goals. Use this routine only as a reference. What matters most is choosing a form of movement that supports long-term well-being. Walking, lifting, stretching, surfing or swimming, or simple daily activity all serve the same purpose when done consistently. The goal is to build a routine that fits the life you have today while supporting the life you want years from now, and allowing room for flexibility as the needs of your life and body change.

Week 1		
	Monday	Chest, front & side deltoids, traps, triceps, abs
	Tuesday	Back, biceps, rear deltoids, abs
	Wednesday	Quads, hamstrings, calves, abs
	Thursday	Functional training with my trainer
		Core, balance, functional work
	Friday	Chest, front & side deltoids, traps, triceps, abs
	Saturday	Back, biceps, rear deltoids, abs
	Sunday	Active rest (hiking, stairs, etc.)

Week 2		
	Monday	Quads, hamstrings, calves, abs
	Tuesday	Chest, front & side deltoids, traps, triceps, abs
	Wednesday	Back, biceps, rear deltoids, abs
	Thursday	Functional training with my trainer
		Core, balance, functional work
	Friday	Quads, hamstrings, calves, abs
	Saturday	Chest, front & side deltoids, traps, triceps, abs
	Sunday	Active rest (hiking, stairs, etc.) *+ 30 minutes of cardio daily, primarily step mill*

Etc.

Our health is an act of service toward ourselves, allowing us to be available when others need support. When we show up strong, rested, clear-headed, and energized, we can support the people who count on us and participate in our communities.

A moment that stayed with me happened after a client-review meeting during a turbulent market week. One of the clients paused before leaving the room and said, "Thank you for taking such good care of yourself so we know you'll be here to take care of us."[2]

It struck me because it was the first time someone connected my own wellness to their sense of security. I've always viewed time in the gym and eating habits as a personal preference. So hearing that it gave someone else peace reminded me that our personal health also influences the people who rely on us.

How many leaders have burned out because they never learned to rest? How many parents can't fully play with their kids because they're too tired? How many marriages have suffered because one partner stopped taking care of themselves (or worse yet, their partner isn't helping them balance the daily responsibilities of the household, so they literally don't have *time* to take care of themselves)?

Taking care of our health is more selfless and generous than we realize. Because when we're healthy, we're available and dependable. We can carry weight, literally and figuratively. And especially in our

[2] The individual quoted above is a client of the firm. No compensation was provided for the statement.

modern world, which constantly pulls at our time and energy, being someone other people can count on is a kind of wealth all its own.

Whether it's taking the stairs instead of the elevator, skipping that extra drink at dinner, or choosing seven hours of sleep over another Netflix episode, those small choices add up.

What Good Is a Fit Body With a Broken Spirit?

You can run six miles every morning, lift more than your bodyweight, and eat like a nutritionist, but if your mind is exhausted, anxious, or detached, your physical shell won't carry you very far.

We've all had seasons where our bodies may have seemed "fine" on the outside, but inside, they've been fried, and where our minds have become brittle. This happens when we chase success, saying yes to everything and pushing harder and faster until, at some point, our bodies say, "Enough." But in many of these situations, it's not our bodies that fail first. It's our spirits.

Short-temperedness, restlessness, being distracted in conversations and distant at home, and our bones feeling heavy, not just our muscles; those are the parts of health we don't talk about enough.

Our mind is the command center for every decision we make. So, if it's clouded with stress, overstimulation, or self-doubt, our choices (even the good ones) start to feel like burdens instead of tools.

Taking care of our health goes beyond the physical workout routine and into the realm of stress management. It's how we talk to ourselves. It's how well we recover from the daily demands life throws at us. And for me, that meant building internal practices that could hold me steady when the outer world was shaking.

For me, it starts with prayer, getting quiet in the morning, grounding myself in something bigger, and asking for gratitude, strength, patience, and guidance before the day begins. Then the routines: journaling, reading, leaving gaps between appointments so I don't live in constant reaction mode, and intentionally carving out silence so my nervous system can breathe. I also sought therapy, which helped me process my past experiences and the narratives they created in my mind, regulate my emotions, and understand how those experiences were informing my present.

And, perhaps most importantly, I began to set boundaries. Boundaries with work, social obligations, screen use, and even perfectionism. I had to redefine what "enough" looked like so it no longer was dictated by the concept of output.

Burnout stems from ignorance of mental health. But many of us struggle to recognize the signs of burnout, especially when we're trapped under the social pressure to keep pushing through. It's important to check in with ourselves and look for common signs of overreach, such as rising irritability, shallow breathing throughout the day, evening cravings, mindless scrolling at night, and a calendar with no empty space.

I'm not a medical expert, so this is just my opinion, but in my experience, if three or more of these signs are present for a week, it might be worth reducing your overall load and increasing the amount of rest you get.

It starts as exhaustion, but it ultimately becomes disconnection. We start forgetting why we're doing what we're doing and lose empathy. We lash out or shut down. We go through the motions in our relationships. And before long, the people closest to us begin to feel like strangers.

Mental health is health. There is no separation. Our brains live in our bodies. Our emotions affect our hormones, digestion, sleep, and immunity. Our stress levels are tangible and measurable. And if we don't manage them, they *will* manage us.

That's why I take sleep seriously. Nothing good happens after 10:00 p.m. Our bodies heal at night, and our minds process and recharge. If we're going to war with our alarm clock every morning, something's broken upstream. And sleep deprivation doesn't just make us cranky. It impairs decision-making, slows our metabolism, weakens our immune system, and increases our risk of anxiety, depression, and chronic illnesses. There's no badge of honor in being tired all the time; that's just personal neglect.

Rest is productive. Specifically, it's one of the most powerful tools in your health arsenal. Yet it's the first thing most people sacrifice. And I get it. We're conditioned to *do*. But none of us can operate effectively and produce the output expected of us when we haven't slept enough and taken care of our physical and mental health needs. When we rest, we come back sharper, kinder, more patient and understanding, and more present. Rest helps us avoid mistakes and allows us to make better decisions.

Our team doesn't need us to be impressive. They need us to be *well* (which, ironically, is impressive).

And that goes for our families, too. Our kids don't care about our status. They care if we're home. And when we're home, if we're actually there instead of scrolling or being distracted or emotionally unavailable. That kind of presence takes energy, and energy comes from wholeness.

So, here's your challenge: start treating your mental and emotional health like the core of your wealth instead of an accessory.

- Protect your sleep, because your performance depends on it.
- Say no to one thing this week that drains you.
- Write down what you're grateful for every morning.
- Reach out to a therapist or coach to start investing in yourself.
- Breathe deeply. Often, and intentionally.

Start listening to your body, your thoughts, and your patterns.

Longevity and Living Like It Matters

Becoming a parent changes your perspective on everything, especially your health.

When I had my first daughter, Nicole, I was younger. My body took to late nights with a newborn and long days at the office alongside my workout routine more effectively. My energy seemed endless. I wasn't thinking long-term. I was thinking, "Get through the day." Now, though, as an older dad, it's different. Every game of tag, every early school drop-off, every backbend to pick up a toy, I feel it. But I also value it more. Because I know I don't have the same physical capabilities as I did in my twenties. And I don't take a single moment for granted.

In my thirties, I could grind and still function. I could skip a few nights of good sleep and still lift heavy. I had a margin. But in my sixties, I protect everything. I protect my morning routine. I protect my recovery. I protect my peace. Because my body is the only place I have to live. I can't trade it in or take a vacation from it. And the quality of my life (not just the years, but the living) will be determined by how I care for it.

And that applies to everyone. It doesn't matter if you're in your mid-twenties or late fifties, or whether you're a stay-at-home parent or a high-powered executive, these principles apply to every person, at every stage of life, on every budget. Just because we "can" survive by coasting or without addressing our physical and mental health, that doesn't mean we should. And living in those ways robs us of experiencing life to the fullest.

Here's what I know works:

- Move your body daily. It doesn't matter if it's walking, stretching, lifting, dancing, or swimming; just move.
- Eat real food. Minimize the processed stuff. Add more colors to your plate and stick to ingredients you can pronounce.
- Sleep for seven to eight hours.
- Get sunlight whenever possible. Your circadian rhythm and mood rely on it.
- Reduce screen time, especially before bed. Your mind needs time to wind down.
- Limit electronic frequency exposure. Unplug your Wi-Fi at night and keep devices out of your bedroom.
- Hydrate. Half your body weight in ounces is a great start. Water is life.

These are simple, but they're not always easy. But what matters is that they're attainable goals that can become new habits when discipline is engaged. Forget the newest fitness and wellness apps. You need consistency. You need to remind yourself, every day, that the choices you make right now are building (or eroding) the future you're going to inhabit.

I'll leave you with a few questions. Don't rush past them. Sit with them, and be honest.

What good health habits have you abandoned (or avoided)? And why? What's one thing you can do today to take care of your future self? What story are you telling yourself about your health? And is it helping or hurting you?

You're not too old. You're not too busy. You're exactly where you need to be to start. So, start small. But start today. And if you've already started and stopped, *start again.* Your health is the fuel that lets you build everything else. Set it up as the foundation for the rest of the pillars so they have stable ground to build on top of.

With the body supported and the mind quieter, our attention can turn to the people who make a life rich. The next chapter explores why family and friends are the net worth that compounds when everything else fluctuates.

Family & Friends: The Real Net Worth

"A friend loves at all times, and a brother is born for a time of adversity."
Proverbs 17:17

No one on their deathbed says, "I wish I'd worked more." I'm sure you've heard this sentiment before, but the reason it's repeated is because it's true. I've sat across from clients in their sixties, seventies, even nineties, and they've never once celebrated the weekends they spent in the office. They've never lit up talking about how many hours they billed or how many emails they answered after dinner. When people are honest with themselves, they don't measure their life in work accomplished. They measure it in the people they loved and the relationships they either invested in or let slip away.

Regret and resentment often show up in those reflections. Regret is quieter, like an ache we carry because we wish we'd done things differently. Resentment is louder. It's the bitterness that builds when we feel like we were shortchanged or robbed of something we deserved. Yet both teach the same lesson: family and friends are the real net worth. So when those relationships suffer, no amount of professional success can fill the hole.

There was a period in my life when business (or rather, busyness) consumed me. Meetings stacked on top of meetings. My travel schedule and workout routine would keep me out of the house. I experienced constant pressure to hit numbers and keep clients happy. And it didn't exactly help that, for many years, I was in a toxic marriage with my first wife, which made me even less motivated to be home and present. But I told myself it was all for my two children at the time, and that the hours I poured into work were an investment in stability and opportunity for them. But there were moments when the very people I claimed to be working for (my own children) felt my absence more than they felt my love.

If time is our most precious asset, who was I really spending it with? Not my kids. Not my friends. I was spending it at work with things that didn't hug me back or ask me how my day was.

In the early 2010s, somewhere between 2011 and 2013, I decided to take some classes and really learn about wine beyond wine tasting being a casual passion. It was during those classes when I thought, "If I keep doing this, maybe I can become a Sommelier." That's when I really got into it. My daughter Tehani, hadn't been born yet, so there was a window of opportunity at that time which I wouldn't have later while raising a newborn. Studying for the exam meant poring over my notes for hours on the weekends, using our master bed to spread all my papers and flashcards and maps out across it.

One particular Sunday, two days before the test, I was hours into my study session when Tina came into the room crying. I immediately asked what was wrong, and she said, "Are you having an affair?" The question completely threw me off. I'd become so focused on passing the test, it didn't occur to me how she might interpret the endless hours in which I locked myself away to prepare for it. She, understandably so, felt neglected and wasn't sure why.

All that effort paid off in the end. I passed the exam on the first attempt, which isn't easy to accomplish. But more importantly, I was reminded of the delicate balance between my relationship with productivity and my relationship with my family. Both are important, but we need to be careful not to pour all of our effort into one zone, accidentally forsaking the other.

Health prepared the foundation. This pillar plants what lasts. Energy without connection becomes nothing but a performance, and connection without energy collapses under stress. But when both are present, life holds steady through hard seasons.

Early Lessons in Dysfunction

To understand why this lesson has been so important, not just in my own life but also in the lives of other people, we have to go back to where I came from. My childhood home wasn't a model of healthy family dynamics. My father drove long-haul trucks, so he wasn't home much, but even when he was, there was a physical and emotional distance. And my mother carried a temper that could flare up without warning. Explosive is the word that fits best. Arguments happened suddenly and intensely, leaving behind an atmosphere of volatility and unease. And when they were both home together, my parents often fought with each other.

In that environment, family didn't feel safe. It felt like a place where you braced yourself for the next blow-up or letdown. And as the oldest child, I was forced into a sort of protector role, whether I wanted it or not, let alone whether I realized it. Which meant growing up faster than I should have, carrying responsibilities that weren't mine, and learning to survive in a house where trust was fragile and love often came with strings attached.

Those lessons dug deep. They taught me conflict management, but not the healthy kind. They taught me survival, but it was survival built on hyper-vigilance. They taught me loyalty too, but a kind of loyalty based on fear of abandonment. And most of all, they taught me distrust. Of authority, of intimacy. Distrust of promises that people made but didn't keep. Those were the things I carried into adulthood, and they shaped how I approached relationships later on, which is why I stayed in my unhealthy marriage for as long as I did.

When you grow up in dysfunction, you don't leave it behind just because you move out of the house. You carry it with you, like an extra shadow that follows you into every new relationship. But I didn't realize this for a long time. I thought I was different, that I was choosing a new path, but the patterns repeated. I found myself drawn into dynamics that echoed what I'd known as a child, and my options became arguments that escalated too quickly or sucking up toxic behavior purely to avoid getting into arguments.

It took years to see the pattern clearly. Years of wondering why I kept ending up in the same place and thinking it was always the other person, without realizing I was bringing my own unhealed wounds into the equation too. And don't get me wrong, the things my ex-wife put me and our children through weren't okay. But I made the choice to stay for as long as I did. Dysfunction begets dysfunction until you stop, name it, and do the hard work of breaking the cycle.

That's why I say I didn't know what a healthy family looked like. I had to unlearn old lessons and teach myself new ones. I had to redefine loyalty as showing up consistently for the people who matter. I had to learn that survival mode doesn't build intimacy, and that conflict doesn't have to destroy connection. I had to learn that trust can be built, but only when both people are committed to honesty and accountability. And these were things I had to construct brick by brick after watching the walls collapse.

Regret, Resentment, and Responsibility

I regret the times I let work eclipse time with my children. I regret the nights I was physically present but emotionally absent, distracted by stress or exhaustion. I regret the milestones I missed and the memories I didn't help make. I regret not taking myself and my at-the-time two children out of a toxic family dynamic sooner. But those regrets fuel me now. They remind me not to take moments for granted and not to trade being physically *and* mentally present for productivity.

Resentment, though, is trickier. I carried resentment toward my parents for the instability of my childhood. I carried resentment toward my first marriage for the dysfunction I became trapped in. And sometimes, I even resented myself for staying too long, for not drawing boundaries sooner, and for repeating patterns I swore I'd never repeat. But resentment can eat away at us if we let it. It can harden our hearts, closing us off from connection and convincing us that isolation is safer. I've had to work hard to release resentment, to forgive where I could, and to set boundaries where I couldn't, and to take responsibility for my own role.

At some point, you realize that your past may explain why you do the things you do and who you've become, but it doesn't *excuse* anything. I could spend my life blaming my parents for their volatility or my ex-wife for exhibiting qualities similar to those of an addict, but that doesn't change that I choose how I show up in my relationships. Which means that I have to take responsibility for breaking patterns, for being intentional, for choosing connection, and for prioritizing people.

One Brick at a Time

When I say I had to build family and friendships from scratch, I mean it in the most literal sense. I didn't have a plan for what "healthy" looked like. I had examples of what *not* to do, but I had to experiment to figure out what *to do* instead. I had to learn that being a father meant more than providing financially and sharing surface-level experiences; it meant being present emotionally and showing up when it was inconvenient or messy or even when it cost me something. And I had to learn that being a partner meant more than staying together.

I stumbled. I fell short. I repeated old mistakes before I realized I needed new tools. But over time, I started to see the difference. I started to feel what it meant to be part of relationships that gave more than they took. I started to experience the *wealth of connection* tied to love built on respect instead of fear. And that's when I understood what people mean when they say family and friends are your true net worth. Because without them, the rest of life feels empty. But with them, even the hardest seasons feel survivable.

Take a moment and think about your own story. Where do regret and resentment show up in your relationships? What milestones have you missed, and what would it look like to show up differently moving forward? Who in your life do you need to forgive because *you* need to be free from the bitterness? What patterns from your past might still be shaping the way you build relationships today?

You don't have to have it all figured out. You don't have to inherit a perfect model of a family or friendship. You can build it yourself. But you do have to make that choice and follow through. And once you do, you'll realize the same thing I eventually did: that on their deathbeds, people often wish they'd loved better and built the kind of wealth that no one can take away.

Blood Doesn't Always Equal Family

There's a difference between having relatives and having what I call relational wealth. Relatives are the people you're tied to by blood or circumstance. You don't choose them, and sometimes you wouldn't even if you could. Relational wealth, on the other hand, is made up of the people you invest in and who invest in you. They're the people who see you fully, who walk with you through both celebrations and crises, and who remind you that life isn't meant to be carried alone.

I've got thousands of "friends" on social media. In fact, the last time I checked, I had well over 4000 Facebook friends. The number sounds impressive, but it's hollow. Out of that list, I can count maybe five people who I know, without a doubt, would show up if I called them at 2:00 a.m. And those five people don't need a "like" button or an algorithm to prove their loyalty. They've proven it through years of consistency by showing up when it wasn't convenient, and knowing my flaws but sticking around, anyway.

There's a quiet joy in having friendships that stretch across decades. These are the people who know your story because they've lived parts of it alongside you. They know your history because they were there when it happened. They've seen the good seasons, the ugly seasons, the confusing in-between seasons, and they didn't run.

I think of a couple of my closest friends. The ones who didn't flinch when my first marriage unraveled, and who didn't pull away when I was emotionally messy. There's no performance in these kinds of friendships. You can be vulnerable without worrying it'll be used against you. You can share your doubts without fearing they'll redefine how you're seen. That kind of friendship lives in the background, steady and sure, like a heartbeat you don't notice until you stop and realize you wouldn't survive without it.

Long-standing friendships are rare, especially in today's digital age. They take work. They take sacrifice. They take a commitment to consistency. But when you find them (or more accurately, curate them), they're worth more than any amount of money.

Nurturing Friendships

But maintaining these friendships isn't easy, especially when life gets busy. Careers, marriages, parenting, health issues, relocations; they all conspire to squeeze friendship into the margins. If you're not careful, months slip into years, and you wake up realizing you don't even know what's going on in your best friend's life anymore.

Friendships (just like familial relationships) don't survive on autopilot. They need intentionality. That means scheduling time instead of waiting for it to appear and picking up the phone instead of just scrolling through updates. Plan that coffee, that dinner, that surf session, and share that bottle of wine, even when you're tired, even when it feels like one more thing on the calendar. Because if you don't prioritize friendships, the busyness of life will always push them to the bottom of the list.

They also need vulnerability. Small talk is fine, but real connection happens when you're willing to go deeper. When you admit you're struggling. When you share the fears you usually keep hidden. When you let someone else see behind the curated image presented in boardrooms and on social media. Vulnerability creates trust, and trust is the backbone of true friendship.

And then there's consistency. Not every interaction has to be deep or groundbreaking, but there should be an ebb and flow between the profound, soul-exploring stuff and the little things. A quick text, a funny meme, a "thinking of you" call. Consistency says, "I'm still here. I still care. You still matter." Making time in your schedule is just the first step. But if every time you meet up with that person, the quality of time spent together is flat and lackluster, neither of you will walk away feeling like the time was worth it.

Those three qualities (intentionality, vulnerability, and consistency) are the habits that turn acquaintances and "gym buddies" into lifelong friends and strengthen the bonds we have with our families. And in the wealth equation of life, they're some of the best investments you'll make.

My First Marriage …

… lasted nineteen years. Eighteen years longer than it should have. From the outside, we looked like a family holding it together. Two parents raising kids and keeping the machinery of daily life running. But behind closed doors, our life together was a trash fire.

In my opinion, she had aggression issues, which weren't always contained to private situations. Trying to talk with her about her struggles just risked more incidents. And codependency stood on both sides of the relationship: she needed the financial stability I offered through my career, and I clung to the quiet desperation of trying to hold it all together for the kids. I told myself staying was noble, that sacrificing my happiness was worth it if it meant my children had two parents. But kids can feel dysfunction even if you think you're hiding it, which is something I should've known after my own experiences with my parents. They see the tension. They hear the fights. And in some ways, that's more damaging than separation.

I spent nearly two decades in that marriage trying to make it work. I hoped counseling would change things, and believed my patience would pay off. I told myself I could absorb the dysfunction without it spilling over onto the kids or into my professional life. But it all just kept getting worse until I couldn't handle it anymore.

Therapy taught me that to protect myself and my kids, I couldn't allow her to be physically abusive toward me. So, one night, I finally called the police. At the time, it was one of the hardest things I'd ever done. Admitting that my marriage had descended into something bad enough to put my then-wife behind bars felt like failure. But I'd reached a breaking point. She was arrested, and I was granted a restraining order. And just like that, the life I'd tried so hard to hold together cracked wide open.

Divorce is never easy, especially after nineteen years and with children involved. But staying even longer would've been harder. I chose to finally leave not only for myself but for my kids. I wanted them to grow up knowing that love is supposed to feel safe. Walking away was an act of self-preservation, but it was also an act of love for my children and for the version of myself that deserved better.

That season taught me more about relational wealth than any business deal or transaction. It taught me that not all relationships are worth preserving, and that sometimes the most loving thing you can do *is* walk away. Family isn't defined solely by blood or marriage but by the quality of connection, safety, and respect.

It also taught me that loyalty in relationships doesn't mean tolerating dysfunction. It means having the courage to demand better and set boundaries to protect yourself and the people who depend on you.

Those are lessons I carried forward into every relationship since, and why today, I have a beautiful relationship with my now-wife, Tina and our young daughter, Tehani.

Relational wealth involves learning from pain and choosing not to pass it on. about it demands deciding that the cycle stops with you, whatever cycle that may be, and actively choosing to build relationships that matter.

Think about your own circle of relationships. Who are the people who bring you emotional wealth? Who are your five real friends, the ones you can count on when everything else falls apart? What small steps can you take this week to be more intentional, vulnerable, and consistent in nurturing those friendships?

Then, ask yourself some harder questions: are you holding on to relationships that drain you more than they nourish you? Are you sacrificing your well-being in the name of keeping the family picture intact? Are you staying in environments that are unsafe or relationships that are unstable, hoping things will change, while teaching your children that dysfunction is normal?

Family and friends are our real net worth, but only if those relationships are built on trust and respect. We don't need thousands of Facebook friends. We need a handful of *real* friends who will walk into the fire with us. We don't need to hold on to a marriage or a relationship just because it looks right on paper. We need the courage to create connections that are truly right in practice.

Relational wealth is built choice by choice and boundary by boundary. And every step we take toward healthier relationships is a step toward a wealth that'll outlast anything money could buy.

Finding Hope Again

The end of my first marriage left me shattered in ways I hadn't anticipated. It wasn't only the loss of a spouse or the upheaval of divorce. It was the unraveling of dreams I'd invested almost two decades into. When you give that much of yourself to a relationship, and it ends in toxicity, it can leave you questioning everything: your judgment, your worth, even your capacity to love again.

But healing is possible. It just doesn't happen overnight, and it doesn't happen without work. For me, the healing process began with therapy. Sitting across from a professional who could help me untangle the patterns I'd carried since childhood was uncomfortable at first, but therapy forces us to hold a mirror up to our lives and confront the ways we've repeated dysfunction instead of escaping it. And it made me examine not only my ex's role in the breakdown of the marriage, but also my own. How had my childhood shaped my expectations? How had my need to protect or fix blinded me? How had my tolerance for volatility kept me in a relationship long past the point of no return?

Therapy gave me tools I'd never been taught and helped me set boundaries, recognize red flags, and believe I was worthy of more. Rebuilding trust started with myself. Only then could I begin to imagine trusting someone else.

It would've been easy to grow cynical. To decide that relationships weren't worth the risk after everything I'd been through. But deep down, I didn't want to live that way. I still believed in love, and I still believed in partnership. But I had to do the inner work first. I had to give myself permission to heal before I could give myself permission to hope.

And then, when I least expected it, serendipity stepped in. I initially met my current wife, Tina, in passing as I walked into a restaurant. But three years later, I met her again, this time at a film festival. It wasn't a place I thought I'd meet someone significant, but sometimes the most important connections happen when you're not looking for them. We struck up a conversation, and there was something about her presence—warm and grounded—that caught me off guard.

That moment was the beginning of a second chance at a real partnership. With Tina, I didn't feel like I had to perform or protect, but that I could simply be myself. And that was enough.

Seasons of Life

As I mentioned earlier, one of the starkest contrasts in my life has been raising kids in my twenties versus raising a kid in my fifties. In my twenties, I had energy to spare. Sleepless nights were easier to bounce back from. I could chase my kids around the park, juggle work and parenting, and still find time to surf or hit the gym. But I was also immature. I was still figuring myself out, still carrying the baggage of my upbringing, and still trying to deal with my first marriage.

By the time I became a father again in my fifties, everything had changed. My energy wasn't the same. Sleepless disruptions hit harder. And the physical demands of parenting were more taxing. But the trade-off was wisdom. I'd lived through mistakes. I'd missed milestones before and knew better than to take them for granted. I'd learned that no success at work was worth the regret of being absent at home.

The birth of my youngest daughter was one of the most impactful experiences of recent years. She came after years of trying and hoping. And by the time she arrived, I'd already raised two children to adulthood. I knew what it meant to hold a newborn, but this time it felt different. It felt like … grace. It felt like a gift I didn't deserve but had been given, anyway.

Being an older dad brought both joy and fatigue. There were moments of overwhelming gratitude (like watching her take her first steps, hearing her first "I love you," and seeing her personality unfold). But there were also moments when I felt the weight of my age. Keeping up with her boundless energy was exhausting. And always, in the back of my mind, was the awareness that my time with her was finite in ways it hadn't felt in my twenties.

But that awareness sharpened my commitment. You don't get to go back and fix missed moments. So, with Tehani, I refused to make the same mistake. I wanted to be there whenever possible. I wanted to build memories she'd carry with her long after I was gone.

My son, Christian, also added a new layer to how I think about family. Years ago, when I was at the Monarch Resort with my daughter, Nicole, and grandkids, I met a young father while we stood in the wading area with our toddlers. A little later, his sister-in-law, Emily, walked by. Something about her presence struck me. Christian had been struggling to find the right partner, and in that moment, her energy felt like a match for him. But I knew it would be awkward to approach her myself, so I asked Nicole to make the introduction. And Nicole tried, but the message came out in a way that left me embarrassed and laughing about it later.

But even with that clumsy start, Emily shared her number. Nicole showed her a photo of Christian, and they agreed to meet the following weekend. Yet, before that day arrived, they crossed paths by chance at a small Mexican restaurant in Laguna. Emily recognized him from the photo, stepped outside to gather her courage, and walked back in to introduce herself. That became their first real conversation, although they still met that Saturday as planned, spent the day at the beach with her sister's family, and ended the evening at a backyard barbecue. Their connection grew from there.

Fast forward to when they eventually decided to marry; they asked me to officiate. I became ordained online and reached out to the pastor who'd married Tina and me. He shared his ceremony structure, which I adapted to fit them, and that was that. The wedding was simple and intimate, held on the sand with only the parents present, but it didn't matter how many people attended. Standing there with them felt like an honor. It's one thing to watch your child fall in love. It's another to be asked to stand inside that moment with them.

One of the greatest lessons I've learned through these seasons is that family isn't just who we raise. It's who we rise with. Blood may define relatives, but family is defined by commitment and by the people who stand with you in the trenches, lifting you when you stumble and celebrating when you succeed.

With Tina, I've experienced what it means to *rise with* someone. We've faced challenges together, from the fatigue of parenting later in life to the complexities of blended families, and through it all, we've chosen each other. That choice, made daily, is what makes a family strong.

Signs of Relational Wealth

So, what does relational wealth look like in practice? It looks like the kind of trust where you don't second-guess motives or fear betrayal. It looks like the kind of safety where home is a refuge instead of a battlefield. It looks like the kind of joy found in laughter around the dinner table or quiet evenings on the couch. It looks like situations where burdens are shared and people are becoming better versions of themselves because of the relationship, not despite it.

That's the kind of wealth no economic downturn can touch. It's the kind of wealth that makes everything else in life meaningful (and ties heavily into the Invisibles, which we'll explore more later).

Take stock of your relationships right now. Are you still carrying wounds that keep you from trusting again? What steps would it take for you to begin healing? Who in your life has shown up, like Tina has for me? Have you acknowledged them, invested in them in return, and appreciated them? And if you're a parent, how are you showing up differently with your kids now compared to earlier in life?

What does relational wealth look like for you? Who do you *rise with*? Who are the people who make your life rich in meaning?

Healthy Boundaries

Family and friends are some of the richest assets we have, but not every relationship belongs in the portfolio. Some connections add value, fill us with energy, and remind us why life is worth living. But others drain us, chip away at our confidence, or even pull us backward into dysfunction we've worked hard to escape. Part of building relational wealth is learning to evaluate which is which, and setting boundaries or walking away when necessary.

For years, I believed that family was sacred no matter what, and that blood ties obligated me to endure toxicity and excuse behavior that would never have been acceptable from anyone else. But eventually, I realized that being family by blood or marriage isn't a free pass.

Some of the hardest boundaries I've had to set have been with relatives. People who shared my last name but not my values. People who expected unconditional access without offering respect in return. For a long time, I tolerated it because I thought I had to. But you're allowed to decide that toxic relationships don't get a front-row seat in your life.

But walking away doesn't always mean cutting someone out completely. Sometimes it means redefining the terms of engagement, or limiting contact, or choosing not to engage in arguments, or protecting your peace by refusing to be baited into the same old patterns. Other times, it *does* mean a complete separation and acknowledging that proximity is too costly.

That decision is painful. It's never easy to admit that someone you love is also someone you need to step away from. But boundaries are an investment in the relationships that deserve your time and energy, not a punishment of the ones that don't. As for what those boundaries should be and what they should look like, that depends on the relationship. The kind of boundaries we have with our partner won't be the same as those with our children or friends or co-workers. And which boundaries need to be in place in those relationships depends on what each of us needs. Just remember, boundaries aren't about telling other people what to do but informing those around us about what *we* will do based on how we're treated by them.

Investing in the Right Relationships

If toxic relationships drain you, healthy ones sustain you. But sustaining them takes intentional investment. In the same way, you wouldn't expect your financial portfolio to grow without attention, you can't expect your relationships to become stronger and last if you neglect them.

As we touched on earlier, one of the simplest, most effective investments is scheduling connection time. Or, more specifically, *quality* connection time. And just like with boundaries, what is considered quality time is unique to each of us and our relationships. Life is busy, and if you wait for the perfect moment to appear, you'll be waiting forever. Put family dinners on the calendar. Block out time for date nights. Schedule trips with friends. Treat those commitments with the same seriousness you'd treat a meeting with your most important client, because this is how you'll receive the real wealth of life.

Another investment is unplugging. Our devices constantly compete for our attention. It's easy to sit at the dinner table physically present but mentally absorbed in emails, or scrolling through social media. Choosing to unplug (e.g. leaving your phone in another room, closing the laptop, turning off notifications) sends a message that the other person matters more than the screen.

Then there's the courage to apologize first and forgive fully—within reason. Relationships aren't perfect. We hurt each other, sometimes intentionally, though often not. And waiting for the other person to make the first move only prolongs the distance. Apologizing first requires humility, but it opens the door to reconciliation. And forgiveness allows both people to move forward by choosing not to let resentment rot the relationship.

Don't underestimate the power of small gestures, either. Send the text. Make the call. Drop a note in the mail. Show up at the hospital. Drive across town for coffee. Too often, we tell ourselves we'll reach out "someday." But someday isn't a date on the calendar. And those small investments compound over time, creating bonds strong enough to withstand anything.

One of the greatest regrets I hear from people is waiting too long. Waiting to reconcile. Waiting to say "I love you." Waiting to spend time together. Waiting until retirement to travel, until the kids are grown to connect, until the schedule slows down to prioritize relationships. But relationships don't wait. *Life* doesn't wait. And if you keep putting love on hold, one day, you'll find that all the opportunities have passed.

At the end of the day, relationships are what remain. Money fades. Careers end, and eventually, achievements are forgotten. But the people you've loved and the people who've loved remain in your heart.

Relationships ask for an anchor when emotions run high and seasons shake the ground. The next chapter explores that anchor. It looks at belief, prayer, and purpose as stabilizers that help relationships hold on a soul level.

Faith: The Anchor in Every Storm

"Now faith is confidence in what we hope for and assurance about what we do not see."
Hebrews 11:1

What keeps you grounded when everything else shakes? There are seasons when the ground under your feet feels steady, like when our careers are on track, our marriages are stable, our kids are doing well, and our health is manageable. And then there are seasons when everything shakes at once.

There was a time in my own life when clients were demanding, markets were unpredictable, and I was stretched thin by trying to keep everything afloat while also trying to deal with my toxic first marriage. Add to that the responsibilities of parenting, where my kids needed me present and patient even though I felt absent and exhausted, and it was chaos from every angle.

In those moments, the usual anchors didn't hold on their own. Work didn't give me peace. Success felt hollow, regardless of who I was doing it for. I didn't have the time or energy to work on my relationships.

My own strength wasn't enough. The only true steadiness I found came from prayer and faith.

There were a few points in my life when faith stopped being a concept because it became necessary.

I was in Moorea, Tahiti in 2023. And each day, I would go hiking on a privately owned mountain near our bungalow. On one of those days, Tina asked me to leave my phone behind. She told me to disconnect from the outside world and use the hike as a chance to reflect and recharge. So I left my phone behind and went on my usual hike.

I successfully completed the hike, and the view from the top was breathtaking. The ocean stretched out in every direction; the wind blew gently through the trees, and the silence of the world around me brought a deep sense of peace. It was one of those moments that reminded me how small humans are, in the most positive way.

But things changed dramatically as I began descending, and I hit a patch of red clay. The clay was slick. I lost my footing and tumbled. And as I felt, I felt something snap in my leg. The tendon connecting my quad to my knee tore and my muscle recoiled up my leg.

I lay on my back, staring at the sky, overwhelmed by the pain. I couldn't believe what had happened. Everything seemed so still, aside from the roosters and chickens crowing in the distance. It all seemed surreal, like my body and the world were out of sync.

When I tried to stand, the second I placed weight on my injured leg, it buckled. I fell again, and this is when reality really sank in. Initially, there was fear. Then, for some reason, I laughed. Lying there, I laughed through the pain and thought, "This is how it ends? At the will of the roosters?" The absurdity of it broke through the shock, and I was able to send out a silent prayer.

God. Where I'm at, what's the next thing to do?

About a hundred yards away, I saw a fence. It was the only visible structure anywhere nearby. So I rolled over onto my stomach and pulled myself along the ground using my arms. Every inch was a struggle. It was slow and difficult, but I managed. And when I reached the fence, I used the wire to hoist myself up. Along that painstaking drag, I realized that if I kept my injured leg straight, I could apply some pressure to it, so once I'd hoisted myself up, I started hopping.

It took me approximately one hour to make my way down the remainder of the mountain. Hop by hop. And once I reached the end of the mountain, I crawled across the road to get to the other side.

By the time I returned, what normally takes one hour to hike had taken me three hours. Tina was pacing, worried about what was taking me so long. And once she looked at my face, she immediately knew something was wrong.

After that, it was off to the hospital. I received confirmation of the quad tendon rupture, but I didn't have surgery to fix it until a week later, back in California. But the experience that's stuck with me since isn't the injury. It's the moment on the mountain when, all alone and flat on my back in the middle of nowhere, my only choices were panic or faith.

That's what faith looks like in real life. It doesn't wait until the circumstances are ideal. It emerges when there are no guarantees and no quick fixes. When there's no one else to rely on, faith gives us the ability to keep moving forward, even if moving past the obstacle requires a slow, uncertain process.

Faith is built in moments like this, when control is gone and the next step is not guaranteed.

In contrast, my first exposure to faith felt more like compliance. I didn't get to choose my involvement because it was picked for me by my family. And, at least for me, the messages I received during that period often felt guilt-driven.

Still, I went through the motions because that's what I was told to do, even though I didn't feel any personal connection to God or any form of higher power at the time. I just didn't want to do the "wrong thing," instead of focusing on the kind of faith that would be meaningful to me personally.

By the time I was nineteen, I'd walked away from the practices my family chose for me. Not from God Himself, just from the version of Him I'd been presented. I didn't turn my back on belief. And I wasn't insulting any religion; I was merely deciding that their teachings weren't for me. And that decision opened the door for me to explore faith in new ways. It freed me to ask questions, to wrestle with doubts, and to search without fear of punishment. It set me on a path that was less about one specific religion and more about a relationship with God.

Ritual still matters. It gives shape to the act of devotion, but for me, a relationship with God gives it life. The change for me was letting how I wanted to practice my Faith serve that connection. If a ritual deepened my attention to God, I kept it. But if it felt like I was only checking a box, I set it down.

Developing a Personal Relationship

Over the years, that search led me to develop a truly personal relationship with God. It wasn't neat or tidy the way I felt forced into through the church, but little by little, I found ways of practicing faith that felt real to me. And this process was helped along by a close friend (my then-roommate and surfing buddy, Mark) who nudged me toward Christianity overall more than a specific demonization within it.

I began praying in my own words, like a conversation instead of a recitation. Sometimes the prayers were long, sometimes they were short. Sometimes they were eloquent, while other times they were a collection of chaotic thoughts. But they were mine. And in those prayers, I felt a sense of connection I'd never experienced through the faith that had previously been chosen for me.

I started wearing a cross as a simple symbol I could carry with me, grounding me when life felt overwhelming. It reminded me of the presence and strength I could draw on.

I also began attending non-denominational services. And what struck me about those gatherings was the emphasis on a relationship with God. For the first time, I felt like faith was something I could embrace of my own free will and desire, because I was personally choosing the kind of faith I wanted to engage in. I could go directly to God myself to admit my failures, ask for forgiveness, and take personal responsibility.

Embracing personal responsibility also changed how I approached forgiveness. I learned to stop seeing forgiveness as being about the other person and instead about being for *myself*. By taking personal responsibility, offering forgiveness became an act of self-compassion, which released me from the emotional hold other people had over me, regardless of what they'd done.

That's what my Faith has become for me: an anchor. Life is going to shake. Maybe not today. Maybe not even tomorrow. But there will always be something, someday, that will make things uncomfortable and challenging. And it's in those seasons of uncertainty where faith acts as the grounding force.

Faith is about having an anchor strong enough to hold on to when life shakes. And it will. The question is, what are you trusting in, and does it work for you?

Respect Without Agreement

For much of my adult life, I've made a deliberate choice to not broadcast my religious or political views in public, because I've seen how quickly those labels can divide people before a real conversation begins. The moment you lead with a verse or a political party, you risk being reduced to that one identity. People stop listening. They put you in a box, and whatever comes out of your mouth next gets filtered through assumptions and biases.

I've never wanted that. I don't want my Faith or my politics to become accidental weapons that drive people away. I want the way I treat people and extend respect to speak louder than any bumper sticker or social media post. Faith, for me, is something deeply personal. It informs how I live, but it doesn't need to be splashed across a billboard.

Disagreement is often treated as hostility. If someone doesn't share your faith or your politics, the expectation is that you either avoid the subject completely or go to battle. But that mindset robs us of connection by assuming that difference is a threat instead of an opportunity.

But I've learned that respect doesn't require agreement. Some of the people I respect most don't share my Faith, but they've taught me things about discipline or compassion or perseverance that I might not have learned otherwise. And in the same way, I hope I've modeled for them that faith in God doesn't have to mean judgment but that it can be humble and kind and bring strength; I lead by example.

The goal is understanding. The goal is to be able to look someone in the eye, acknowledge that you see the world differently, and still choose to honor the humanity in them. That choice doesn't weaken your faith. If anything, it strengthens it because it proves your faith is big enough to handle differences and the complexity of every person's unique human experience.

Whether It's God or Something Else

One of the most fascinating things I've read is the research on centenarians, people who live past one hundred. Scientists have studied these communities around the world, from Okinawa in Japan to Sardinia in Italy to Loma Linda in California. The diets are different. The daily routines are different. And most of their cultures are different. But one thing all of them have in common is some form of consistent spiritual practice.

For some, it's prayer. For others, it's meditation. For others, it's a rhythm of community worship or daily rituals that connect them to something larger than themselves. It doesn't always look the same, and it doesn't always carry the same theology, but the thread is that *belief in something matters.* Having an anchor that grounds and centers you and a worldview that gives you meaning isn't optional if you want to thrive long term.

What anchors me is God. It's the personal relationship I've built through prayer, reflection, and community. But I don't believe faith only counts if it looks like mine. I've met people whose beliefs are rooted in the universe, in karma, in ancestral traditions, in the simple conviction that there's more to life than what we can measure or control. The point isn't to argue whose belief is "right." The point is that belief itself matters. It changes how we endure suffering and how we celebrate joy, and it changes how we see our role in the world.

Don't get hung up on the labels. Don't disqualify yourself because your faith doesn't look like your neighbor's or your parents' or your pastor's. Ask yourself instead, "What gives *me* meaning? What keeps *me* grounded? What helps *me* endure when life feels impossible?" If you can answer that honestly, you've tapped into the heart of faith.

Take a moment to think about your own life. Do you feel pressure to make your faith or beliefs public, or are you comfortable letting your life be the testimony? How do you respond to people whose beliefs differ from yours? Do you listen without the intention to judge, or without your initial judgements impacting how you treat other people?

What daily or weekly practices ground you and provide you with meaning? Prayer, meditation, quiet walks, journaling; what centers you? And what would it look like to respect someone's belief system without needing to agree or convert?

My Faith has never been more real to me than in the moments when life felt impossible. It's easy to talk about faith when things are going well, when the bills are paid and the family is smiling. But faith isn't tested in the good seasons. It's tested in the moments when everything falls apart, and you don't know how to keep going.

I've lived through many of those seasons. Divorce. Custody battles. Business struggles that left me questioning everything I thought I knew. Each of those moments threatened to undo me. And in each of them, my Faith became the primary thing that gave me perspective. Faith that the pain wasn't pointless, that rebuilding was possible, and that even when I didn't understand the "why," there was still a reason to keep going.

Around the time of my divorce, my then-sixteen-year-old son got into a horrific accident. Unbeknownst to me at the time, Christian was struggling with the circumstances of my divorce, but had figured out how to hide it. He later confessed that all he had to do was call me while he was out and calmly explain that he was just hanging out with friends and all was well, even though he was actually partying. And I believed him, both because I wanted to trust my children and in my having raised them well, and because Nicole had proven a pattern of trustworthiness. His job at the time wasn't impacted. He worked night shifts at malls, converting old stores into new store locations while the mall was closed, which involved him traveling from place and place. So I wasn't able to witness his habits.

When the accident happened, he was working in Maui, Hawaii, and he'd gotten into cliff jumping off Black Rock (where the locals go), which was up at the top, where the drop is a few hundred feet. He and his friend had both been drinking before the jump, so he had less control over what his body was doing as he plunged toward the water. And however he hit the water, the impact stopped his heart.

After one to two minutes of Christian not re-emerging, his friend dove in to search for him. And by the time he found my son and struggled to drag him to shore, Christian hadn't been breathing for ten or eleven minutes. Which should have been a death sentence. If it hadn't been for the vacationing paramedic from New Zealand who'd been nearby when it happened, Christian might not be here today.

That morning, being three hours ahead of Maui's time zone, I woke to a slew of missed calls and messages from Maui Memorial Emergency, informing us that Christian was in critical condition and they weren't sure if he would wake, or if he would, how bad the brain damage would be.

After a chaotic rush to get our dogs situated, Tina, myself, and Nicole (who was still breastfeeding her baby at the time) flew to Maui, clueless about what state we would find him in. When we arrived, he was hooked up to a bunch of machines in a coma. It didn't look promising.

Meanwhile, what we didn't know until later, word got around the area that a young tourist was dying in the hospital, and the locals had started a prayer circle on Christian's behalf.

Seven days after being admitted to the hospital, he woke up—but he woke without any lung or brain damage. It was something that scientific evidence couldn't explain. Even the doctor who'd come to check on him couldn't believe it. He left the room, shaking his head and calling it a miracle.

Was Christian saved by God? Or was he just lucky? All I know is, in addition to the local prayers being cast into the universe, before I'd even arrived at the hospital, a friend of a friend named Susan sat by Christian's side for eighteen hours, holding his hand and talking to him. I found out afterward Susan had lost her own son because of a similar drowning accident years before and believed he'd returned to Earth as a sea turtle to help Christian make it back to the shore. Coincidences or not, it was more than enough for me.

Faith is less about answers and more about endurance. While Christian was still unconscious, I prayed and prayed and prayed. I didn't understand why he ended up in that situation, nor how he survived. But my Faith reminded me that my perspective was limited, and so is the perspective of all humans on Earth. I couldn't see the whole picture. But I didn't have to.

That doesn't mean I plaster on a smile and pretend everything is fine. Faith isn't denial. Instead, it's choosing to believe there's a reason to keep going even when the evidence seems stacked against us and to trust that the pain we're in now could one day produce growth we can't yet imagine.

When I look back now, I can see threads I couldn't see then. The divorce forced me to confront patterns I'd avoided for years. The custody battle made me fight for my kids in ways that deepened our bond. Christian's accident allowed me to see the struggles he'd been hiding and be there for him. None of those lessons make the pain less real, but they prove that the pain wasn't wasted. And my prayer and Faith helped me through these times.

There were nights when I lay awake asking questions I never thought I'd ask. Why go on when everything I've built collapses? Why start over when I'm already exhausted? Why forgive when the people who hurt me don't deserve it? My Faith didn't hand me easy answers. What it did was whisper reminders.

> *Go on because your children still need you.*
>
> *Start over because the story isn't finished.*
>
> *Forgive because carrying bitterness will only poison you, not them.*

Faith, at its core, is perspective. It doesn't change what happened, but it changes how you see it. Without faith, betrayal becomes the end of trust. With faith, betrayal becomes a lesson in discernment. Without faith, divorce becomes the end of love. With faith, divorce becomes a chance to rebuild healthier relationships. Without faith, loss becomes unbearable. With faith, loss becomes an invitation to hope.

It's easy to misunderstand faith as having to be dramatic, like burning-bush moments, life-altering revelations, or the kind of sudden understanding that lifts you off your knees and sends you into the world renewed. But that's not how faith usually shows up.

At least, not for me. My Faith became real in the small, everyday moments most people overlook.

Faith shows up in the pause before reacting, when you're frustrated, misunderstood, or overwhelmed, and everything in you wants to fight back or shut down. But instead, you breathe and choose patience.

Faith shows up in the conversations you don't want to have but know you need to have. When you tell the truth instead of protecting your pride, or apologize first, even when you feel justified, choosing connection over being right.

Sometimes faith looks like waking up early even when you feel defeated, whispering a quiet prayer, and trusting that the strength you need will meet you somewhere between the first step and the next.

Faith is choosing to believe that what you're building (with your time, your intentions, your discipline, and your presence) matters, even when progress is invisible. It's trusting that your effort isn't wasted just because the results haven't arrived yet.

And sometimes faith is simply showing up. To your life, to your family, to your responsibilities, to the day in front of you.

I've found that my Faith is what carries me when certainty disappears. It's the steady voice that says, "Keep going. Keep trying. Keep believing. You're not alone."

I don't pretend it's easy. There were days when my Faith felt thin. But even then, it was the string I held onto. Thin as it was, it was enough to keep me tethered and moving forward and reminding me that what feels like the end may actually just be the middle of the story.

Maybe you're in a season like that right now. Maybe you've been betrayed by someone you trusted. Maybe you're in the middle of a divorce, or a custody battle, or someone in your life is struggling in ways you can't fully understand. Maybe you're asking the same questions I asked. Remember, you don't need to have the answers right now. You just need to keep asking the questions in the presence of faith, and trusting that even if you don't see the larger purpose today, one day, you will.

Where do you feel betrayed or broken right now? How might faith reframe that pain into something purposeful? What small step forward could you take, even if you don't understand the "why" yet? Who do you need to forgive because *you* need to be free?

Anchoring the Day

For me, the quiet, faithful moments often happen in the morning. Before emails, calls, and obligations take over, I pause to engage in prayer and gratitude for the fact that I woke up, that I get another shot at this life, or that the people I love are still here. Those moments don't look spectacular to anyone else, but to me, they're sacred. They remind me that I'm not the center of the universe and that something bigger is at play.

Faith, in its simplest form, is remembering we're not alone. It's choosing to believe that even the smallest act of acknowledgment can connect us to something greater than ourselves. Faith is built in both the everyday and the extraordinary. Faith is cumulative. It grows with each whispered prayer, each moment of gratitude, and each surrender in the midst of chaos. It becomes a part of us, and then, when the extraordinary moments come—the ones that test us to our core—we realize that faith has already been built into our foundation.

Try this exercise: write what I like to call a "Statement of Vision." It doesn't have to be long. Just a few sentences that capture what you believe, what you hope for, and what you want to anchor your life around. We'll look at my own Statement of Vision later, if you need a specific example. But first, try writing your own to get your thoughts going. Don't worry about perfection. No one else will hear it but yourself (unless you choose to share it with other people). Just write from the heart about what matters to you and where you want that to take you in life. And once you've written it, speak it aloud every morning for thirty days. See how it changes the way you approach your day. See how it shapes the way you handle stress, conflict, and uncertainty.

When I created mine, it was right before New Years, 2002. I visited my favorite local beach. Along the edge of the sand, there was a grassy hill, and I sat up there all day with a notepad, just enjoying the breeze on my skin and the soothing swish and sway of the waves. Perhaps the setting influenced my Statement of Vision, or maybe my decision to visit the beach that day was driven by the vision already living in my heart, and I just hadn't recognized it yet.

Anchored faith doesn't end in private peace. It moves outward, and the next pillar traces that movement. Service turns belief into action and changes good intentions into lives that benefit other people.

Service to Others: The Currency of Purpose

"It is more blessed to give than to receive."
Acts 20:35

Why spend time volunteering when you could be earning more? Because life should be about more *meaning*, not just more money. Some people have genuinely asked me that question. They've seen my schedule, the hours I devote to community work, mentoring, and nonprofit events, and they wonder why I "waste" so much time when that energy could go toward profit. And the answer is, money feeds comfort, but service feeds the soul.

Long before I achieved any kind of financial success, long before I had the means to give in big ways, giving was the one thing that consistently pointed me toward what mattered. It reminded me that success is contributions in addition to accumulation.

There's a quiet kind of fulfillment that comes from helping someone who can't repay you. It strips away ego and status and leaves behind connection. When you give your time, your attention, or your resources without expectation, you tap into a sense of purpose, which will always go deeper than any transaction.

Somewhere along the line, we've been sold the myth that service only counts when it's big. When you're cutting six-figure checks or your name is on a donor wall. And sure, those gestures matter too. Large-scale philanthropy changes lives and communities. But that narrative convinces everyday people that their contribution doesn't count.

I've heard people say, "Once I make more money, I'll start giving back." Or, "When I retire, I'll have time to volunteer." But reasons like that are exactly what stops us from actually engaging in service. You don't need to be wealthy to be generous. You just need to be willing.

Some of the most impactful acts of service don't involve money at all. They involve time, kindness, attention, and care. Such as a neighbor who shovels an elderly couple's driveway without being asked, or the teacher who stays after class to help a struggling student, or the friend who shows up when tragedy hits and doesn't leave. It's not glamorous, nor is it publicized, but it changes lives all the same.

When I think about the times service meant the most in my own life, it always came down to how present I was over how much I could financially give.

I've spent years volunteering for different causes: youth mentorship programs, financial literacy workshops, community outreach events.

And each time, I've walked away humbled by how much I've received in return. Spending time with people who are fighting for better circumstances reminds me of what I don't want to take for granted and helps keep me grounded.

Time is the most valuable currency we have, because it's the one thing we can't get back. When we give our time to others, we're giving something irreplaceable. We're saying, "You matter enough for me to stop my world for a moment and step into yours."

That's the beauty of service. It expands our perspectives. People become real, making them carriers of stories instead of another tick on a statistical chart. They help us realize that our presence can bring relief, encouragement, or hope in ways we might never fully understand.

Giving Resources

Of course, money and material resources also matter. Financial giving can transform organizations and amplify impact. But even then, the heart of service is all about the intention.

Each time I give, I remind myself that resources are meant to circulate. Money, tools, knowledge, even access; these things multiply when shared. The greatest wealth is the kind that flows through you, not the kind that stops with you.

But money and time aren't the only kinds of resources we can offer. We live in an age where everyone's multitasking, distracted, and perpetually busy, making attention one of the rarest forms of generosity. So sometimes, the most meaningful service we can offer isn't writing a check or showing up to an event. It's simply listening. Listening without judgment and without rushing to respond or fix something. Just being present.

I've had conversations with employees, clients, and friends who later told me that a single moment of being heard changed their day or their direction. I didn't offer them advice. Not really. I just showed them that they matter, and they're seen for who they are and what they need.

As a society, we underestimate the healing power of presence. People are starving for it more and more as smartphones and social media have taken over. And they don't always need solutions to the things that challenge or bother them. They often just need someone to remind them they're not invisible.

Meaning Matters More

The beautiful thing about service is that it never stops with one act. We might never see where the impact spreads out to, but it moves outward in ways we can't measure. Consider dominos that've been knocked over; one touches another and that one touches another until the whole line has been pushed over.

It's easy to get caught up in the grind of achievement and to measure success by our income, title, or recognition. But at some point, we realize that the things that fill our bank accounts don't always fill our hearts. Meaning does. Connection and contribution do. When we give—time, resources, or attention—we create meaning that outlasts the moment. We participate in something bigger than ourselves and become part of the invisible network of kindness that holds the world together.

And the irony is, the more you give, the richer *you* feel. Not in the financial sense, but in the sense that your life feels full and more fulfilled. You'll sleep better. You'll stress less. You'll walk with a lighter heart because you'll know you've made someone else's load a little easier to carry.

If you've been waiting for the "right time" to serve, this is it. You don't need to wait for more money, more time, or a grand opportunity. Start where you are.

Ask yourself:

- Who in your life needs your time right now?
- What resource do you have that could make someone else's path a little easier?
- Who needs your full attention? A friend, a child, a colleague? Someone who simply needs to feel seen?
- What message are you sending with how you give? Are you saying, "you matter?"

Every act of service, no matter how small, sends that message. And sometimes, that's all someone needs to keep going. Lives have literally been saved because someone received a smile and a kind gesture on the very day they planned to be their last. You never know what other people are dealing with, and it takes nothing from us to be good to those around us.

How I Serve

Over the years, I've had the privilege of supporting organizations that do incredible work in the community. Each one has a story, and each one has shaped me in ways I didn't expect.

Surf & Turf Therapy has always held a special place in my heart. The organization helps children with autism experience the joy of surfing and horseback riding, something that (for many of them) might have seemed impossible, alongside receiving therapeutic services. Watching these kids, who often face daily challenges with communication and sensory processing, light up when they catch a wave is indescribable.

My exposure to Surf & Turf Therapy came through a longtime employee, Danielle, who volunteers with the organization. She spends her weekends out in the ocean helping children get onto a board, steady themselves, and ride their first wave. It struck me that everyone out there is volunteering their time simply to give a child a moment like that.

That's what service looks like to me: giving someone a moment of freedom, joy, and possibility. And it's why I keep going back to Surf & Turf year after year. Because every time, I'm reminded that generosity restores something in ourselves in addition to helping others.

Two other causes close to my heart are Breakthrough T1D (formerly called the Juvenile Diabetes Research Foundation) and Cure Duchenne. Breakthrough T1D funds research and advocacy aimed at curing, treating, and supporting those with type 1 diabetes. Cure Duchenne works toward treatments and hope for children living with Duchenne muscular dystrophy. Both support children fighting battles they didn't choose, and both represent hope.

Understanding the impact a diagnosis has on families brought the mission into focus for me. It's one thing to hear about chronic illness. It's another to watch parents count carbs, measure insulin, and pray every night that their child's blood sugar stays stable.

Cure Duchenne hit me in a similar way. Duchenne muscular dystrophy robs children of their strength little by little, year after year. And when you meet the families affected by it, you see the quiet courage they live with daily. The parents are warriors, and the children who suffer from this condition are heroes.

Organizations like these remind me that giving is much more about partnership and loving others than pity. Pity shouldn't be the primary reason we serve, even if it might play a factor in our decision to act. Service to others is about linking arms with people who refuse to give up, who keep fighting for progress even when the odds are long.

And supporting them is a way of saying, "We see you. You're not alone."

Another cause that's meant a great deal to me is CASA (Court-Appointed Special Advocates). CASA volunteers step in to represent children in the foster care system, giving them a voice when they often don't have one. Thousands of kids move through the system every year, their lives shaped by court rulings and case files. And many of them have no consistent adult to advocate for them. CASA changes that by training volunteers to be those advocates, to make sure a child's needs and best interests are heard and protected.

For two years now, I've also served as master of ceremonies at the Literary Project's annual fundraising event. The Literary Project helps underprivileged children learn to read, giving them tools for opportunity and confidence.

The Boys & Girls Club, too, has always been one of my favorite organizations because it focuses on prevention instead of repair. It gives kids a safe space to go after school and provides mentors to guide them and structure to help them grow into confident, capable adults. Supporting programs like that feels like an investment in the next generation.

You might have noticed that all of these causes and organizations specialize in helping children. These are the kinds of causes that speak the most to me, but you should choose the causes and acts of service that, in turn, speak the most to you. What kind of things are you passionate about? Animals? The elderly? Children? The education system? The arts? Relationships and families? Use that passion to guide you toward causes you can partner with to make a difference.

How We Serve

Service is a personal value of my own, but it's also a part of my company culture. From the start, I wanted to build a business that measured success by something more valuable than just finances, so we made giving back part of our DNA.

Each year, our team sits down to choose causes to support. Sometimes we pick organizations that align with our values as a company, such as financial literacy, youth development, or health-related causes. Other times, we choose based on what matters to individual team members. If someone's passionate about animal rescue, or veterans' support, or cancer research, we find ways to contribute.

We use three filters. Does this align with our values? Does anyone on the team have a direct connection? Can we support with time, not only with money?

And what's beautiful is that when people are empowered to give, they bring that same empathy, patience, and perspective into their work and relationships.

I've never once regretted giving someone more than they expected, whether it was time, attention, or generosity. This applies to clients, to friendships, and to life in general. Sometimes it's as simple as picking up the phone instead of sending a text. Sometimes it's offering mentorship to a young professional who's struggling to find their path. Sometimes it's donating when there's no photo op or recognition. But every time I've stretched beyond what was convenient, it's come back multiplied in ways that had nothing to do with money.

Giving changes the giver just as much as, if not more than, the receiver.

How Giving Changes You

When you give, you deepen your capacity for empathy. You start to see people differently. You realize everyone has their own story, and that most of them are fighting something unseen. And why wouldn't they? If you have your own experiences, good and bad, of course every other person has their own version of life on their shoulders too. As a society, we just need to consider the world outside of ourselves from time to time to recognize that.

Giving also rewires scarcity thinking. It shifts our focus from, "What if I don't have enough?" to, "Look at how much I already have." Scarcity says, "Hold tight." But service says, "There's more where that came from." And that mindset changes our entire approach to life and business.

And giving creates purpose. It reminds us that our time on this earth means something, and we have the opportunity, every day, to do something that'll leave other people better than how we found them. And wouldn't you want the same in return? Wouldn't you want people to see *you* and consider what your struggles and needs are too?

I've built wealth. I've built businesses. But the most meaningful thing I've ever built is the habit of and love for service.

For a moment, stop and think about the causes or people that move you. The moments that make your heart ache or your spirit light up. That's where your purpose is pointing. What cause do you care about enough to give your time, attention, or resources to? How could you bring others—your team, your family, your friends—into that mission? And where can you give more than expected?

The world needs willing hearts. And the gifts we give to others always find their way back to us, changed, multiplied, and meaningful.

To Those Who've Been Given Much, Much is Expected

True service doesn't come with strings attached. It's not a strategy, a brand, or a tax deduction. It's a way of living that says, "I see you, and you matter," without needing recognition, reward, or applause.

The best acts of service are the ones no one else knows about, the quiet, selfless gestures that impact lives unnoticed. Real giving is unconditional, not based on what you'll get back but on what you've already been given.

A close friend of mine, Moses, taught me more about that kind of giving than anyone else. Moses grew up with very little, and as a young boy, he helped his mother pick berries for a living. He worked hard, eventually built a career, and created a stable life for his family. But even as his success grew, his humility never changed.

Stores like Walmart (among others) used to offer layaway programs, where customers could ask the store to reserve a product for them for a few weeks or months. And during that time, the person could pay off the cost of the product little by little until they'd completely paid for it. While most stores don't do that anymore, back then, Moses would call the Walmart in the neighborhood where he grew up in New Mexico during the Christmas season and ask how much value was still on layaway. And he'd pay it. He would cover the rest of the layaway costs for all the customers currently using the program, so when they'd come into the store again to make their next payment, they'd learn they're free of the financial burden and be able to take the product home. And when Walmart eventually ended the layaway program, he changed his approach and purchased about $30,000 in Walmart gift cards to deliver to local kid's parents.

I spoke to him about ways to get a tax deduction for these gifts, but he doesn't care about that. He's not self-motivated in that way.

That's what service looks like when it's unconditional. Quiet and heart-led. Our modern world makes it too easy for generosity to become performative. And while visibility can inspire others to give, it can also dilute the intention of the act. Performative giving seeks acknowledgment, while heart-led giving seeks impact.

I've been in enough rooms with high-net-worth people to know how easy it is to conflate generosity with branding. And I get it, public giving can draw attention to causes that deserve it and potentially attract more business to a company. But if your motivation is recognition, you're missing the point of engaging in service.

The most powerful moments of giving never make it to social media. They happen quietly, often in private. Similarly to what Moses would do, silent giving could be a client who anonymously paid a single mother's rent for a year, or a teenager who started a food drive without telling anyone, or even an employee who donated vacation days to a coworker battling cancer. Those moments don't trend, but they do change lives.

Quiet generosity has depth. It doesn't need applause because the act itself is the reward. We can walk away lighter yet grounded, because giving in secret frees us from the performance of virtue and lets us experience the essence of it.

Moses's story made me think a lot about the extension effect of generosity. He didn't just help those families financially. He reminded them that goodness and kindness without expectation still exist. And those families will have remembered that act for years because it restored something in them by relieving them of their burden.

Maybe it made them a little more hopeful. Maybe it made them want to pay it forward. That's how generosity works; it multiplies.

Practical Ways to Build a Life of Giving

But not everyone can walk into a store and pay off every layaway account. And to be honest, that's not the point. The point is to build a lifestyle of giving that fits your capacity and reflects your heart. Here are a few ways to start:

1. Volunteer consistently. Start small. Volunteer once a quarter or even once a year. Join a community event. Serve at a local shelter. Mentor a student. Coach a youth team. Consistency is what matters, not the scale. Every hour you give plants a seed of connection somewhere.
2. Tithe time or income. Tithing isn't limited to money. It's about giving a percentage of what you have to something that serves others. It might mean setting aside 10% of your earnings for charity, but it could also mean dedicating 10% of your week to volunteer work. Even a small percentage adds up when it's intentional.
3. Donate with purpose. Most people think of donating as spring cleaning (getting rid of what they no longer need). But intentional giving asks, "Who could this help?" If you're donating clothes, choose items that carry dignity. If you're giving furniture, make sure it's usable and clean. If you're contributing food, give what you'd feed your own family. But before giving, ask one more question: would I feel respected

receiving this? If not, choose differently. Dignity is part of the gift.

4. Teach kids about giving. Involve your kids in service early. Let them pick a charity to support and have them help pack food boxes or write cards for seniors. When children see generosity modeled, it becomes a part of their identity, and they learn that service isn't something to do when they've "made it" but because it makes *them*. We help our clients organize family meetings and discuss family values, gifting, ideas, etc.

Like exercise, the more we do it, the stronger the muscle becomes. At first, it might feel small, perhaps even insignificant. But over time, it shapes how you think, how you lead, and how you love. And when you make giving a habit, it begins to show up in unexpected ways. You'll listen more and notice needs you used to overlook. And the more you give, the more you'll want to give.

Service always comes full circle. The energy we put into the world through kindness and generosity finds its way back to us. Not always in the form of money or success, but in peace, perspective, and connection.

When I think back to Moses, I see a man who understood that truth instinctively. He didn't need to see the faces of the families he helped. He didn't need a thank-you note. He just knew that giving freely was the right thing to do. That's the model I try to live by. Because the older I get, the more I realize that one of the true measures of wealth is in what you give away.

Where can you give without expectation? What would it look like for you to serve quietly, without recognition? How could you build giving into your routine so it becomes part of your rhythm? What example of generosity do you want to set for your family, your team, your community?

You don't have to change the world through a single gesture. You only have to change *someone's world* through one gesture.

Build giving into your rhythm, instead of pushing it aside like leftovers. Don't treat giving as something to do when time allows—after deadlines, after financial goals, after everything else is handled. That perspective is well-intentioned but backward. If you only give what's left over, you'll never give enough. Because there will always be something else demanding your attention, your energy, and your resources. Giving can't live in the margins of your life. It has to live in the center.

Building generosity into our rhythm doesn't mean we have to overhaul everything. It just means we need to plan for it the way we plan for work, family, or fitness. Budget for it. Make space for it. Treat it as a priority instead of an afterthought.

The Rhythm of Generosity

For me, that rhythm started with one simple question: what am I already doing that I could do with more intention? I needed to recognize the opportunities for service already in front of me instead of searching for ones I wasn't already surrounded by. Service doesn't always require a new commitment. Sometimes it just requires awareness.

Consider scheduling generosity into your calendar. That might sound strange, but it works. Once a quarter, maybe volunteer with your team or support a cause you care about. Or once a month, review your family giving plan (or, said another way, what kind of service brings your family joy). Or once a week, check in on someone outside your immediate circle. These intentional decisions create consistency and build a habit of giving.

Don't fall into the trap of, "Once I have more, I'll give more." Because, as we discussed, "more" is a moving target. And what even is "more?" For one person, it might mean making twice the money they need to live for a year. For others, that might not seem like "enough" yet. Which, in effect, makes it always just out of reach. And while you wait, opportunities to make a difference slip by.

Generosity it about availability. And when you stop waiting for ideal conditions, you realize you've always had enough to start.

The people who've inspired me most weren't the wealthiest or most powerful. They were the ones who gave despite their own challenges. The ones who showed up when they were tired and gave quietly without expectation.

Let's make this personal. Someone in your life needs something you already have. It might be your time, your experience, your encouragement, or your attention. Ask yourself:

- Who around you seems weighed down lately?
- Who's struggling in silence because they don't want to ask for help?
- Who could use your mentorship, your listening ear, or your support?

Sometimes, the act of service that changes a person's day—or even their life—just takes intention. A five-minute call. A handwritten note. A genuine compliment. Or a simple, "How are you doing, really?" The most powerful gift we can give another person is to make them feel seen. And every time we do, we reaffirm that people matter more than productivity.

When you think about injustice, struggle, or need, which causes stick with you? Is it children growing up without support? Veterans who need better care? Homelessness? Education? The environment? The things that move you emotionally often reveal where you could contribute practically.

Commit to one act of service this week. Just one. It could be calling someone who's lonely. It could be paying for a stranger's coffee. It could be volunteering an hour of your time. It could be mentoring a student, helping a neighbor, or donating to a cause that matters to you. Don't overthink it. Just act. The beauty of small acts is that they create momentum, so when you act once, you're more likely to act again.

Write your commitment down. Put it somewhere visible and follow through. Then notice how you feel afterward.

The Return on Giving

Service quiets the world and our own problems and offers peace in the knowledge that we helped someone feel just a little better, despite whatever they're going through. It pulls us out of our own heads and puts us back into our hearts by literally changing our physiology. According to a study published through the National Library of Medicine[3], acts of kindness have a relationship with oxytocin, a chemical that boosts mood and lower stress. But even beyond the science, it just *feels* right.

I've never met anyone who regretted giving, but I've met plenty who regretted waiting to give.

The return on generosity is the calm that comes from knowing we've contributed. It's the gratitude that grows when we see how much we already have, and the sense of meaning that helps to ground us when

---

[3] Kucerova, B., Levit-Binnun, N., Gordon, I., & Golland, Y. (2023). From Oxytocin to Compassion: The Saliency of Distress. *Biology*, *12*(2), 183. https://doi.org/10.3390/biology12020183

other things feel uncertain. When we live lives of service, we start measuring wealth by what we share instead of what we receive.

Service creates an impact that outlasts us. Every act of service adds something to the world. And when enough people give in small, consistent ways, entire communities change.

Service isn't something we "fit in" when life slows down. It's something we build into our lives to make them worth living. It connects us to others, grounds us in gratitude, and reminds us daily that our purpose is bigger than our problems. And the reward isn't recognition, but the internal realization that we've contributed to the greater good in whatever way we could.

Or, if I had to sum all this up into one simple concept, I'd say that service is the rent we pay for the privilege of living a life that matters.

Legacy: What Money Can't Buy and Death Can't Take Away

"A good person leaves an inheritance to their children's children..."
Proverbs 13:22

A hundred years from now, we'll be gone. Our cars will be gone. Our watches will be gone. Strangers will live in our houses. So, what from our lives will remain?

That question hits harder as we grow older. We spend our early years chasing things, and somewhere along the way, we start to realize none of them follow us. The car we saved for. The house we renovated. All of it will end up in someone else's hands (at best) or rusting and rotting and falling apart (at worst). It's a humbling thought, but also a freeing one, because if all those things fade, what's left is what matters most.

A legacy focuses attention on the parts of a life that time can't erase: character shown daily and the people shaped by it. So, what part of you can time *not* erase? Your impact and influence. The lessons you taught through how you lived are what stick around long after you.

The word "legacy" has become a bit of a buzzword, but that doesn't make the concept less valuable. Even if you aren't trying to leave anything behind, you do. We all do. None of us can escape leaving some kind of impact on other people and the world (unless we lock ourselves in our houses and never interact with anyone outside of them). So, wouldn't you rather leave an imprint on this world in the best way possible instead of leaving a bad taste in people's mouths at the memory of you? A legacy doesn't form in a eulogy. It forms in our habits while we're still above the ground.

Similarly to the misconception with service, when people hear the word "legacy," they picture big gestures like names on hospital wings, multi-million-dollar foundations, or bestselling autobiographies. And those *are* a kind of legacy, but not the only ones. As we learned, those "loud" gestures often don't carry as much genuine intention as the quieter and personal things.

Think about the teacher who spends decades shaping young minds, or the single mother who raises her children with strength and compassion. Those are legacies, and some of the most impactful legacies are invisible to the outside world. They live in how people treat each other, how they work, and how they love, and they're passed down through behavior and belief more than wealth or status.

When my time is up and other people talk about me, I don't want them to list my accomplishments. I want them to remember how I made them feel, that I've been a good husband, father, and grandfather, and how I showed up for others, even for (if not especially for) those who couldn't offer me anything in return.

Intentional Living

Building a legacy doesn't happen by accident. Or rather, it can, but letting our legacy happen to us instead of creating it intentionally is exactly how either the memories of people fade into nothingness, or history books end up with severe warnings about not making the same mistakes in the future. A properly crafted legacy is the result of small, consistent decisions.

You can't leave a legacy you didn't live.

Try this activity: write one sentence each evening that answers, "What story did today tell about my values?" Keep a week's worth on one page. At the week's end, circle one moment to repeat and one habit to retire.

Every day, we're teaching people what matters to us through how we spend our time, how we respond to stress, and how we treat others. Every interaction adds to or subtracts from the legacy we're building. That realization changed the way I approached daily life, and the way I handled my business decisions became part of it. The way I raised my kids, love my wife, treat my employees; all of that became a part of it too.

Leaving a meaningful legacy requires intentional living. We have to define what we want to be remembered for before the world defines it for us.

What values do you want people to associate with your name? What kind of energy do you want to leave in a room when you're gone? What lessons do you want your children—or team—to carry forward? Once you answer those questions, you can align your choices with your purpose, which builds consistency and trust.

We can turn on the news or scroll through social media and see people (even our own government officials) who believe that having a legacy means working themselves into the ground to leave their kids money. But wealth without wisdom gives people tools they don't know how to use, and all the time pumped into building those resources will ultimately have been for nothing.

You're leaving a legacy today, whether you mean to or not. The question is whether it's one you'd be proud of. The details don't matter as much as the intention behind them, because with the right intention, you won't do things that go against genuine morals and ethics, anyway.

Money can build institutions, but character builds people. And the ways we impact one another are what endure. If you want to measure the concept of your legacy, look at how people live *because* of you. Are they more compassionate, more confident, more courageous? That's a true measure of success.

Intentional living takes discipline through small, repeated actions. Following through on promises. Apologizing when you're wrong. Showing kindness when you're busy. Practicing gratitude daily. Staying consistent with your values even when no one's watching. Those things might seem small, but over decades, they add up.

We can't fake a good legacy. People might buy into an image for a while, but over time, all of our characters reveal themselves. We either live what we preach, or we don't. And our legacy exposes the truth. So, live the story you want told.

Take a moment to think about what you want your name to mean long after you're gone. If someone were to tell your story fifty years from now, what would they say? What would you hope your children or colleagues learned from how you lived? Are you building that story today, or are you leaving it to chance? The answer to those questions shapes everything that follows.

Learning from Flawed Parents

But to understand what we pass on, we first have to look at what was passed to us. The lessons, the pain, the examples—good or bad—that shaped how we see the world. Because a legacy isn't created in a vacuum. It's transmitted through patterns.

What we inherit forms our default. If we grew up around scarcity, we might cling to money or live in constant fear of losing it. If we witnessed volatility in relationships, we might avoid conflict at all costs, or escalate it too quickly. If affection was withheld, we might struggle to express affection toward other people. These internalized experiences shape how we handle stress, success, intimacy, authority, and responsibility. And unless we examine them, we repeat them.

Awareness creates choice. Without that awareness, our legacy becomes automatic and determined by everything but ourselves. But with awareness, our legacy becomes intentional. The values we model, the habits we normalize, the way we handle disappointment, the way we speak to our spouses, the way we respond to pressure; all of it becomes instruction for the next generation.

Whether we mean to or not, we are always teaching. And our true legacy begins the moment we decide which parts of our inheritance to preserve, and which parts to rewrite.

My own legacy began in a house that was far from perfect. As we touched on, my parents were complicated people. They loved in their own ways, but they also struggled. Our home was a mix of chaos, hard work, and unspoken lessons about survival. And although I didn't realize it at the time, those early experiences were laying the foundation for the person I'd become.

My parents didn't give me a model of what I wanted my adult life to look like, but they gave me a model of perseverance. They showed me that even when the world doesn't give me much, I can still keep going.

My mother was fiery, determined, and unpredictable. She could be explosive one minute and affectionate the next. She carried her own traumas and survival instincts, which might have come from living in Europe through World War Two, and often came out as control or chaos. But beneath all that volatility was a woman who hustled to keep us afloat while my father was constantly on the road.

We didn't have a lot, but she made it work. I only found out once she passed away that she used to hide money—literally hide it—around the house. Rolled bills in drawers, envelopes taped under furniture, stuff like that. We discovered she'd stashed around $20,000 in cash, scattered across years of living in constant uncertainty. Of course, $20,000 in our modern economy isn't even a living wage for a year, but it was her way of controlling what little she could. And this discovery told me two things: she never trusted the system, and she always found a way to survive.

Throughout my childhood, she also took on side work. She'd leave early, come home late, and rarely complain. And maybe it was because of all the work she did on the side that she struggled to get a fulfilling and healthy breakfast onto the table each morning, and why she smoked. She wasn't someone who talked about "grit," but she lived it. And looking back, I can see how much of that rubbed off on me. Her version of love might have been messy, but her work ethic was unwavering.

As a long-haul truck driver, my father was gone for days or weeks at a time. And when he was home, the atmosphere in the house changed.

Sometimes it became calmer, sometimes more tense. But even with the distance, his work ethic left an impression too. He'd come home exhausted, covered in road dust, still smelling of diesel and coffee. His hands were calloused, his back ached, but he knew the value of work.

It took me years to understand that love looks different depending on where we come from. My dad's love was quiet. My mom's love was volatile. Both were incomplete. But together, they taught me that I could choose how I wanted my love to be brought into the world and how I wanted to be loved in return. And that lesson became the backbone of my adult life, even considering how much I had to untangle from that history to create a more functional life and family for myself later.

Hardship does something to us. It burns away illusions and teaches us to adapt. It makes us resourceful. And growing up in dysfunction forces us to learn how to read moods, when to speak, and when to stay silent. A skill set that became invaluable later in business, leadership, and relationships.

Emotional stability wasn't a part of my childhood, but I grew up with exposure to extremes. Which gave me empathy for struggle. It made me aware of how fragile stability can be, and how much work it takes to build it. But when you've seen chaos up close, you either repeat it or you rebuild from it. And while initially I accidentally started repeating it, once I became aware of that and made the decision to change, I chose to rebuild.

I didn't want my kids to grow up guessing whether they were loved or safe. I wanted them to know without a doubt. But breaking cycles is hard. I couldn't just *wish* to parent differently. I had to unlearn everything I grew up with.

When Nicole and Christian were born, I was still figuring out who I was. I was young, ambitious, juggling career growth, marital stress, and all the unresolved tension I carried from my own upbringing. I made mistakes. And plenty of them. I wasn't always patient. I wasn't always present. But I learned how to provide connection, not just financial and emotional security.

Raising Nicole and Christian was one chapter of my life. Raising Tehani is another entirely. With the first two, I was in my twenties and thirties. I was driven, impatient, and trying to balance ambition with responsibility. With Tehani, I'm in a different season. Older, hopefully wiser, and definitely slower to anger.

When you parent in your fifties, your perspective changes. Tehani's birth was both a miracle and a reset. She reminded me of what matters most. And as I already mentioned, being an older dad comes with its own mix of joy and fatigue. I don't have the same energy I did at thirty, but I do have more patience. I don't rush through bedtime stories or skip conversations because I'm "too busy." And when she runs into my arms or asks me questions about life, I see the impact of everything I've learned.

We can't rewrite the past, but we can write a better example for the future.

Perfection is a Lie that Kills Presence

Parenting taught me that consistency (and building habits through that consistency) is the rope that ties all these pillars of True Wealth together. You don't have to be the perfect parent. In fact, there's no such thing as being a perfect parent. It's not possible to achieve. You just have to be *present*. Kids don't remember your speeches, but they remember your tone. They remember how safe they felt around you, and whether you looked up from your phone when they spoke.

Now, don't get this confused with the always-on mentality social media has programmed into us. Being present doesn't mean you're always available. It means that when you *are* there, you're *there*. You're listening, engaged, and connected instead of splitting your attention with one eye on your phone constantly. This is something I work on every day, and it's one of my most challenging pillars.

And being honest is a part of being present. Kids need to see you struggle, apologize, and try again so they can have models of that behavior for themselves.

Looking back, I've come to accept that I'll never get it all right. None of us do. But the goal is to keep showing up regardless of our mistakes and imperfections. When I was younger, I equated strength with never showing weakness. Now, I understand that vulnerability is one of the strongest things you can model. In fact, some of the best conversations I've had with my kids started with me admitting I was wrong. That honesty builds trust, and trust becomes the foundation on which they build their own lives. And that's how cycles end.

We don't raise kids. We raise adults who'll raise others. So, we need to prepare them to handle it with strength and grace.

I wanted (and still want) my children to grow up with empathy and discipline. To know how to work hard, but also how to rest. To know how to earn, but also how to give. To know that failure doesn't define them unless they allow it to, but that it can be used to work toward success. And when Tehani has her own family someday, I hope she'll pass that forward, just as my eldest children have. And from them to my grandchildren. And great-grandchildren.

That's the true test of legacy, when what you've taught continues through lives you'll never see.

My parents didn't give me a perfect example. But they gave me the raw materials. And now, I get to pass that on differently through intention, presence, and a love that's consistent, even when life isn't.

Building the Model You Wish You Had

It's easy to build success. It's harder to build *successors*. But that's what legacy work is about. Raising not only your children, but the next generation of thinkers, leaders, and citizens who'll take what you've built and carry it further.

Every good leader starts by leading themselves. Then they lead their family. Then they lead their community. The order matters, because if you can't lead with humility and compassion at home, it doesn't matter what title you hold in public.

Being the kind of parent your kids want to become requires living in a way that earns their respect without demanding it, and being approachable enough that they come to you with problems instead of hiding them (something that even I dropped the ball on during my first run of parenting). My job isn't to make my kids' lives easy. It's to ensure they're equipped and teach them the values that'll outlast me.

But this kind of legacy doesn't *stay* in the family. Or rather, it shouldn't remain just within the walls of your own house. It should be replicated with everyone around us, from friends to co-workers, and even strangers.

I've always believed that when we reach a certain level of success, our responsibilities shift to lifting others alongside ourselves. Or, sometimes, even above ourselves.

Leadership is less about authority and more about influence. Titles fade, but influence doesn't. That's why I try to lead my team the same way I try to lead my family. I want them to leave the organization with more knowledge, but also more confidence and empathy. Because if I've done my job right, their success won't stop when they walk out the door.

Ask yourself, what do you want people to feel when they interact with you? What will your employees, clients, or friends say about how you made their lives better? How are you investing in others so they can carry forward what you've learned?

When people wait until later in life to think about legacy, they miss the most important part: the time to live it. And then, they have no control over how people remember them, and what they did after they're gone.

The Two Directions of Legacy

Legacy flows in two directions. Vertical legacy is what you pass down to your children, grandchildren, and family. It's generational, like a baton you hand off through example and education. Horizontal legacy is what you pass on to your peers, team, or community. It's the influence that spreads outward. And both matter.

Vertical legacy grows through consistency rather than grand gestures. Things like predictable family rituals, an apology spoken with sincerity, or a lesson shared during difficult seasons give the next generation a framework for how to live. These moments teach responsibility and compassion. They also lower the burden on future generations by giving them examples instead of theories.

Horizontal legacy expands through presence, reliability, and shared accountability. From a leader who invests time in teaching others, to a business owner who models fairness even when no one asks for it, to a neighbor who builds connection within a community; they all leave an imprint. And these actions change the standard for how people treat one another.

If you focus only on vertical legacy, you risk raising insulated success (people who succeed individually but never contribute collectively). If you focus only on horizontal legacy, you risk burnout and disconnection at home. The goal is to balance both.

But balancing both directions requires awareness. When life gets busy, it's easy to lean on one dimension and neglect the other. A strong vertical legacy with a weak horizontal reach creates a private life that seems firm, but a public life that doesn't impact anyone. A strong horizontal legacy without a grounded home life creates a reputation built on output instead of genuine substance. A sustainable legacy sits in the middle and brings alignment between who you are in private and who you are in public.

One practical way to monitor this balance is to review which stories people repeat about you. At home, are the stories about presence or absence? At work or in the community, are they about contribution or avoidance?

People remember the effort to improve, the willingness to repair, and the desire to leave people stronger than they were found. So when those efforts accumulate, they create something money can't buy and time can't erase.

Living the Legacy Before You Leave It

A lot of people focus on achievement when they think about leaving a legacy, such as what they built, created, or owned. But most people won't remember what you did. They'll instead remember how you did it and how you treated them.

Intentional living is what gives our legacy its weight. We can't fake it. We have to live it daily, in the small things that no one sees, because how we do anything is how we do *everything*. The small decisions—how we speak to our spouses, how we treat our employees, how we respond when someone makes a mistake—reveal our true character.

Whenever the day comes, you want your eulogy to speak about the time you showed up when no one else did, or the advice you gave when someone needed direction, or the way your laughter filled a room. No one will care about the awards you achieved or the credentials you accumulated on your CV, so put in the effort to be the kind of person who impacts those around you in a way that makes them reminisce, instead of reading out your LinkedIn profile.

Practice kindness until it becomes instinct. Practice discipline until it becomes a part of your identity. Practice generosity until it becomes a reflex. Think of it like compound interest. Every positive action, every act of service, and choice rooted in integrity compounds over time. The longer you live it, the greater its impact grows. And just like compound interest, small contributions make the biggest difference.

Someday, someone will tell your story. They'll summarize your decades of life in a few paragraphs and a couple of quirky or funny tales. That idea should motivate you. Because if someone else is going to write that story, you want to give them good material to work with.

When I think about the people I admire most, their legacies were about what they embodied. They were generous, even when they didn't have much. They were kind, even when life wasn't. They were consistent, even when no one was watching. And those qualities outlive titles, awards, and possessions.

Our stories will outlive us, but we're the ones controlling the direction the plot will take.

Take a few minutes to think through these questions honestly:

1. What stories about your life do you want your grandchildren to tell? What lessons do you want passed down around kitchen tables decades from now? Do you want them to say you worked hard? That you loved deeply? That you treated people fairly? That you never stopped growing?
2. What actions are you taking now that contribute to a legacy you can be proud of? Are you living in alignment with what you say matters most? Or are there areas where you've drifted? Be honest.

3. If you were to write your own obituary today, what would you want it to say? Not what you think others would say, but what *you* want it to say. Would it speak of impact, love, growth, and integrity? Or would it read like a resume?

Writing your own obituary might sound morbid, but it's a powerful exercise. It forces you to face the gap between intention and action and shows you where you're already aligned and where you still need work. And once you see it, you can start living differently.

If you've made mistakes (and you have; we all have), you're not disqualified from leaving a meaningful legacy. In fact, your mistakes might become the most powerful part of it. If you wake up tomorrow and start living with greater kindness or purpose, you're building your legacy. You don't have to undo your past. All you need to do is use the past to redefine your present and move into the future.

Consider the age-old tale of Scrooge, or the other holiday classic of the Grinch. Both of these stories are examples of how, with intentional decisions that are followed through on, we can rewrite the prior legacy we might have been building for something better.

At the beginning of this chapter, I asked, a hundred years from now, what will remain? Now you know the answer. What will remain is everything you gave and shared, all the examples you set, the acts of courage you modeled, and the lives you've touched without realizing it. Those are the things death can't take. The rest will fade. But the way you made people feel and the values you passed on, those will keep moving through the world long after you're gone. So, live accordingly.

At the end of your life, your legacy won't be the size of your bank account. It'll be the size of your impact. Define your worth by how you live *right now*.

Peace: The Wealth of a Quiet Mind

"Peace I leave with you; my peace I give you…
Do not let your hearts be troubled…"
John 14:27

There was a day when it all hit me at once. The phone wouldn't stop buzzing. Emails poured in faster than I could read them. A client had a crisis that "couldn't wait." My youngest, Tehani, needed help with homework. My older daughter, Nicole, was struggling with something she wanted to talk to me about. And Tina had a crisis that needed my attention. All while I was taking client meetings. And somewhere between all of it, I realized I hadn't eaten since breakfast.

By the time the sun went down, I was running on fumes. I sat at my desk, surrounded by awards, framed photos, and financial statements; all the visible signs of a life that was supposed to mean I'd "made it." But I didn't feel successful. I felt spent.

My thoughts wouldn't stop racing. *You forgot that call. You still need to send that report. You're failing as a parent. You're losing your edge.* The noise in my head was louder than any meeting, call, or argument

I'd had that day. And in the middle of that chaos, I asked myself, "Where's my peace?"

For most of my life, I thought peace was something we earned after we've achieved everything else. Once the business is stable, once the kids are okay, once the house is paid off, then peace would come. But peace doesn't show up after success. It's what allows us to sustain success without losing ourselves. I'd spent decades learning how to generate results, but I hadn't yet learned how to regulate my mind.

The truth is, we can have everything we've ever wanted and still feel like our lives are out of control. We can sit in a luxurious office and still feel trapped in our own thoughts. We can check every box society gives us and still lie awake at night asking why we're not happy. That's what happens when we build literal wealth without building peace first.

Peace doesn't come from our environment. It comes from within *ourselves.*

It doesn't fall into your lap because circumstances finally align. It's the byproduct of discipline, self-awareness, and boundaries. It's the result of learning when to stop, when to say no, when to rest, and when to protect your own energy.

Peace is skilled self-regulation. It's attention, breath, and boundaries working together so your actions match your values, even when put under pressure.

A lot of people misunderstand peace. They think it means silence, laziness, or avoidance, or that it's about escaping life's challenges or pretending they don't exist. But real peace is none of those things. You can be in a noisy room and still feel calm inside. Silence can help us focus, but it doesn't guarantee stillness of mind. It's not about doing less, but doing what matters most. And sometimes peace means taking action, while other times it means stepping back.

For me, as a parent of both adult children and a younger daughter, a grandfather, and a husband, and someone who works daily with employees, advisors, and clients, and they all want a piece of me; I'm still trying to find my balance and maintain my own sense of peace without sacrificing the relationships and responsibilities I have with and to all these people in my life.

Peace doesn't mean we stop caring, but it requires us to stop clinging. We can love deeply, work hard, and still stay centered. Peace gives us the distance to care without collapsing under pressure. It doesn't ignore pain or problems, but empowers us to face them without losing ourselves in them.

But the biggest misconception about peace is that it's the same as control. Real peace is knowing what's worth our energy and what isn't and being able to pause before reacting. It demands emotional regulation (the ability to feel anger, disappointment, or grief without letting it dictate our next move), and being present in the moment (the ability to be where our feet are, instead of replaying the past or rehearsing the future). Peace means our actions match our values, and our decisions reflect what we actually care about.

When we build peace from the inside, we don't need everything around us to be perfect. We just need to know who we are and what we stand for.

Bart experiencing peace in Moorea

The Anchor

Storms don't warn us before they hit. They show up uninvited in the form of arguments, a loss, or an unexpected change. But if you've built your peace, you don't need to fear the inevitable storms of life because you know how to anchor yourself despite them.

Money might buy external comfort, but only peace gives you internal comfort.

As I started paying more attention to trying to find my anchors and claim my peace, I had to make small changes. I stopped checking my phone the moment I woke up. I scheduled time to unplug, even if it was only for a few minutes. And I learned to pause before responding to stress instead of absorbing it. Those simple choices didn't eliminate the chaos of life, because that's literally impossible to accomplish, but they changed how I moved through it. I began treating peace like an investment; something that needed consistent deposits of time, attention, and self-respect. And slowly, the racing thoughts slowed. The constant irritation faded, and I stopped reacting out of fear.

And the more I worked on my inner peace, the more I realized how rare it is in a world obsessed with "more." Most people chase the next milestone, believing happiness is one achievement away. But peace comes when we stop chasing and choose to make active choices. Instead of trying to prove our worth, we should learn how to honor our limits. Saying no is a form of self-respect (and respect to those around us, by avoiding promising more than we can offer).

And taking time to rest is mandatory, because if we don't schedule time for our mind and body maintenance, our minds and bodies will *demand* it when they need it—which is usually at the most inconvenient time.

Now, whenever life feels like too much again, and it still does sometimes, I return to the question, "Where's my peace?" And every time, the path back looks the same: slow down, breathe, simplify, and focus.

The Cost of a Chaotic Mind

A chaotic mind is expensive. It drains energy, damages relationships, and destroys our ability to understand the world around us.

I've lived that cost. There were years when I was successful by every external measure, but inside, I was running on fumes. I woke up anxious, went to bed restless, and spent the hours in between snapping at people who didn't deserve it. My patience wore thin. My focus fractured. I was irritable with my kids, distracted in meetings, and short-tempered with employees. I convinced myself it was "just stress," a part of being driven and a consequence of dealing with my toxic marriage at the time. But it was chaos.

And the chaos wasn't *outside* of me. Or rather, it wasn't *exclusively* outside of me.

When our minds are chaotic, everything in our lives follows. We make poor decisions because we're reacting instead of responding.

We damage relationships because we're not present when people need us. We burn out because we never pause long enough to recharge.

It's easy to think burnout is caused by too much work, but it's actually caused by too little recovery (and don't confuse rest and recovery with *sleep*, because they aren't the same thing). A restless mind is like a machine that never powers down. It overheats, breaks down, and takes everything connected to it with it.

Consider, what's the point of building something if you can't slow down long enough to enjoy it?

In my early business years, like many of us do, I equated success with speed. I thought if I worked harder, longer, faster, I'd eventually earn peace as a reward. But that was a lie. And one I had not only convinced myself of, but one our society perpetuates. Look at advertisements, which promote concepts of happiness *connected to products or services.* But peace doesn't come after you achieve everything, or pay for that new iPhone you don't actually need because you already got the new model last year. It comes when you stop sacrificing your well-being to chase everything.

There was one year in particular when my company was expanding rapidly. Revenue was climbing, and the media started taking notice. From the outside looking in, it seemed like everything I'd worked for was finally paying off. But my life outside the office was crumbling. My then-marriage was strained and abusive. My relationships with my kids were thin because of the issues between me and their mother. I barely saw my friends because I was never fully off the clock. And even when I was home, my mind wasn't. I'd be at the dinner table thinking about a client meeting, or on vacation answering emails. And I told myself it was temporary, that I'd slow down once things "settled." But things never settle when our identities are tied to being busy.

Your sleep will suffer. Your appetite with vanish. You may even become more and more reliant on coffee or other stimulants to keep up with the socially expected hustle culture. And all of this will compile into steadily bigger issues.

Health, Relationships, and Longevity

We can't separate peace from health. The body keeps score of every unresolved stress, every sleepless night, and every gritted jaw. And when our minds are in overdrive, our bodies follow. Cortisol spikes and fatigue becomes chronic. We start to normalize exhaustion until it's our default state. That's where I was headed; successful on the outside, but deteriorating on the inside.

And it doesn't just cost us physically. It costs us relationally, too. People start walking on eggshells around us because we so easily lose patience with our spouses, kids, colleagues—everyone and everything. We justify it as "pressure" or "responsibility," but it's really disconnection.

Without peace, we can't connect deeply with anyone, not even ourselves. And we can forget about longevity. Stress shortens our lives, in addition to shrinking the quality of the years we have.

The people who live longest, research shows[4], aren't the ones with the most resources. They're the ones with the calmest hearts, the strongest relationships, and the ability to manage stress gracefully. So, when I finally clued in to how little attention I was giving my capability for peace and peace of mind, I started changing how I lived, one habit at a time.

The first place I found peace was in the morning. That's when I started waking up earlier to become more grounded before the world woke up. At 3:30 a.m., the house is dark and still. There are no emails, no calls, nothing to distract me. It's a sacred time, and that hour became my sanctuary. I'd start with prayer, meditation, and gratitude, then move into a workout, and the repetition of movement and focus on the physical instead of what's trapped in my brain became a form of meditation in itself. It's a way to tell my body and mind that I'm in charge by literally taking charge.

When I pray, I don't follow a script or ritual. I just talk. I listen. I express gratitude, and sometimes I ask for strength. But sometimes, I also sit in silence. Then I visualize, but not in the way "manifestation"

[4] Mineo, Liz (2017). Harvard study, almost 80 years old, has proved that embracing community helps us live longer, and be happier. https://news.harvard.edu/gazette/story/2017/04/over-nearly-80-years-harvard-study-has-been-showing-how-to-live-a-healthy-and-happy-life/

is often talked about online. I see myself moving through the day with composure and calm. It's a kind of mental rehearsal that changes how I show up, and by the time the rest of the world wakes up, I've already centered myself.

Another major change was learning to disconnect. I started turning off my internet and phone notifications before bed. At first, it felt uncomfortable, as if I were missing something important. But what I was really missing was rest. The brain never relaxes when it's always expecting another ping or crisis. So, I made a rule for myself to not look at any screens after 8:30 p.m. Instead, I read, reflect, or talk with my wife. Or sometimes, I sit outside and listen to the night. It's amazing how much better you sleep when your mind knows it's allowed to stop.

Peace also required me to start saying no, often and unapologetically. For years, I said yes to a lot of things. Most opportunities, every meeting, many favors. I thought saying yes made me generous, but it actually made me scattered. Every yes is a withdrawal from our peace account. And if we don't monitor those withdrawals, we'll go bankrupt. Now, I evaluate commitments through one filter: does this align with my priorities and allow me to sustain my peace? If not, I decline.

Politely, of course. But I stick to my limitations and boundaries, and in return, I model that behavior for those around me. Most people feel they have to say yes to everything because they've been convinced by an endless number of CEOs that that's "how you become successful." But we're sabotaging our capability of becoming truly successful when we sell ourselves out to everything tossed our way. By modeling the act of taking our time and energy and peace into our own hands, we give the people around us permission to pause and look at their own capacity too.

I also learned the value of breathing. Yes, you read that correctly. Just *breathing*. It sounds basic, but for someone who lived in a constant state of urgency and hyperawareness of my environment, learning to breathe properly was a game changer. Now, when I feel tension building, I stop and breathe using the box breathing method:

Four seconds in. Hold for four. Six seconds out. Repeat four times.

Deep breathing lowers cortisol and slows the heart rate, bringing the nervous system back into balance. And that small pause between inhale and exhale is where peace hides.

As these practices became habits, I changed how I moved through life. I stopped rushing to fill silence, and replaced it with listening more. My thoughts became clearer, and my relationships deepened. Peace didn't remove the challenges, but it did help me learn how to meet them.

Business still has problems. Life still has drama. But now, when I sense chaos creeping back in, I go back to the basics:

- Move my body early.

- Disconnect at night.
- Say no when needed.
- Breathe through stress.
- Pray before reacting.
- Visualize peace before the day begins.

I used to think the loudest person in the room had the most power. But it's actually the calmest person who does. When our minds are quiet, we make better decisions. We connect more deeply and see opportunities others miss because they're too distracted to notice. Peace gives us that edge. And it multiplies. The calmer we are, the calmer the people around us become.

Peace Is a Practice

It's easy to mistake peace as a trait some people are born with. The calm ones. The patient ones. Those who never raise their voice or lose their cool. I used to envy people I perceived to be like that. Until I learned that peace is what you practice, not who you are.

We don't have to be "naturally zen" to live a peaceful life. We don't have to be inherently religious or spiritual, either. We just have to be willing to work for it.

Peace takes repetition. It's built through habits, awareness, and constant recalibration. Some days we get it right, but some days we don't. And that's okay. It's like physical fitness. You don't stay strong because you worked out once. You stay strong because you keep showing up, even when it's inconvenient or you don't "feel like it." Peace works the same way.

You practice it every time you pause before reacting, every time you listen instead of defending, every time you forgive instead of fighting. You practice it when you slow your breathing during an argument, and when you choose not to send that angry text, or to walk away from a conversation that only drains you. Those moments are small, but they build the inner muscle for peace.

The next lesson I learned was that peace has to be protected. Because once you start building it, you'll notice how quickly the world tries to take it from you. Sometimes it's through obvious stressors, like work, deadlines, or unexpected crises. But other times, it's through relationships that drain you more than they feed you.

Not every relationship belongs in every season of our lives. Some people are meant to grow with us, while others are meant to teach us something and move on. The key is learning which is which.

When a relationship consistently costs you your peace, and conversations never lead to change, learn to walk away. You've tried, you've communicated, and now, if you stay, all that's left is chaos.

On the other hand, when tension comes from misunderstanding instead of malice, learn to lean in and become curious. Some relationships are worth the hard conversations. If there's mutual respect, effort, and care, lean in and work through it. Peace sometimes means staying, listening, and rebuilding.

As for when to let go of fixing it all, this one took me the longest to learn. We can't heal everyone. We can't force people to grow at our pace, and we can't make them see what they're not ready to face. Letting go doesn't mean we stop caring. It just means we stop carrying what isn't ours. It's not our job to manage everyone's emotions. It's our job to manage our own.

And yes, I know protecting our peace gets complicated when it involves family. There's an unspoken rule that we "have to" tolerate family behavior, no matter how damaging it is. But being related doesn't mean being entitled to someone's energy, as we discussed in the relationships chapter. And some of the hardest boundaries I've set were with people who shared my last name.

In the case of my ex-wife, that meant a complete separation, physically and legally. But for others, it might just mean learning to engage differently.

We can love someone and still limit contact. We can forgive and still refuse to participate in old patterns. We can care without being consumed. Peace demands intelligent connection instead of blindly sticking to someone because we're "supposed to." And when we stop letting guilt dictate our boundaries, we create room for genuine love to grow.

The Myths

Despite the misconception, peaceful people aren't conflict-averse. They don't run from hard conversations. They don't turn every conversation into a war because they don't need to win arguments, opting instead to seek understanding.

When we're clear about who we are and what we stand for, we don't need to shout or prove anything. We simply express truth without aggression, and absolve ourselves of the responsibility for the other person's emotions.

True strength is quiet confidence. It's listening without taking everything personally, and standing firm without losing composure.

Another piece of peace is learning to accept time, or rather, to stop fighting the natural rhythms of life. For a long time, I resisted slowing down. I saw rest as weakness. I pushed my body, my mind, and my schedule beyond what was sustainable, as a lot of people in corporate America have gotten used to doing. But over time, peace taught me that energy changes with the seasons of your life.

I don't have the same drive at sixty that I had at thirty. And that's normal. My priorities are different now. I still work hard, but I also protect my recovery. I still aim for excellence, but I no longer chase the false concept of perfection. Peace means embracing your current capacity instead of resenting it or comparing your capacity to other people's.

There's a quiet relief that comes when you stop performing. When you stop needing to prove you're right, or trying to save everyone or rushing to stay relevant. It's easy to mistake the concept of "always being on" as the cost of leadership, but it's actually the fastest path to burnout. The people who lead well, love well, and live well aren't always running. They know how to rest, reset, and reconnect.

So, if "hustling" isn't how we ultimately attain peace, how do we practice peace daily?

By noticing. Notice when your body tenses. Notice when your breathing shortens. Notice when you start rehearsing arguments in your head. Those moments are the cues to pause and breathe. Peace is found in awareness. We can't control every situation, but we can control how we meet those situations when they strike. And every time we choose stillness over turning something into an unnecessary battleground, we strengthen that muscle.

There's no "arrival" when it comes to peace. You don't master it once and move on. You need to maintain it every day. Some mornings, I wake up calm and centered. On other mornings, my thoughts and heart start racing before I slip out of bed. The difference now is awareness. I catch it sooner and realign faster.

Every time I breathe through conflict, every time I set a healthy boundary, I'm investing in my inner wealth. And over time, that investment compounds into a life that feels lighter and steadier.

Learning to Be Okay with Enough

As we touched on in the first chapter, our modern world rewards constant doing. "More" has become the measure of success. More money, more followers, more growth, more goals. Nothing is ever enough. But at some point, "more" starts taking away more than it provides by stealing rest and blurring the line between ambition and addiction.

But there will always be another mountain to climb. And not every season is for summiting. Peace isn't quitting the climb. It's knowing when to rest to be able to continue climbing afterward, and learning that some seasons are meant for recovery and rebuilding instead. We don't have to sprint through every moment of our lives. And sometimes the most productive thing we can do is pause.

"Enough" doesn't mean becoming complacent. It means being *content.* It means realizing that fulfillment comes from appreciating what we already have. We can still hope and dream and wish and set goals. In fact, we *should.* Never stop dreaming and developing. But our happiness and peace need to come from the here and now, or we'll never have peace and happiness in the future, no matter what we achieve.

When we stop needing "more," we finally start noticing the now.

Once I started slowing down, I needed to remind myself not just what I wanted to achieve, but also who I wanted to become. That's when I started creating what I now call my Statement of Vision. Remember that activity from earlier? It's a written and spoken affirmation of the life I'm building based on what I intend to live into. It centers me and helps me focus my energy.

A few of the statements I've used over the years are:

> "I'm in perfect health."
>
> "I have one hundred clients I love to serve."
>
> "I walk one mile on the beach on my ninetieth birthday, hand-in-hand with my wife."

Another example that's already become fulfilled in my life comes from 2002. I wrote down that I have a vacation home that my whole family uses. And since 2023, I now have a vacation home on the island of Moorea to share with those I treasure most deeply.

The key is to write each thing down as if it has already happened.

And along with my Statement of Vision, visualization has been one of the most practical tools for protecting my peace. When we visualize outcomes, we create mental pathways for calm and confidence before challenges even arise. Before a difficult meeting, I'll picture myself speaking clearly and staying composed. Before a stressful week, I'll imagine moving through it with focus and balance. Before I fall asleep, I'll visualize the kind of peace I want to wake up with.

The mind doesn't always know the difference between real and rehearsed experience (a sentiment shared by many self-help books, such as *The Power of Positive Thinking* by Norman Vincent Peale), so the more you visualize peace, the more natural it becomes to live it.

That's why having a Statement of Vision is so valuable. It connects faith to action, and intention to reality, allowing us to start embodying what we seek before it's technically even arrived in our lives.

Faith in Action

People often separate faith and peace as if they're different things. But to me, peace is faith in motion, and the belief that even when life feels uncertain, we can still move with purpose.

Every morning when I speak my vision aloud to myself and take time to focus on the kind of peace I want to experience throughout the day, I'm practicing that belief. I'm reminding myself that that's something I have to actively participate in. And when life inevitably tests that anchor, I come back to my statements. They remind me of who I am and what I'm building, even when circumstances change.

The beauty of this practice is that it doesn't take long. A few minutes in the morning, a few affirmations spoken with intention; that's enough to change how you carry the day. Peace doesn't demand hours of meditation or isolation. It grows in the small, steady rituals that ground you.

Some mornings, I pair my vision statements with breathwork. Other mornings, I repeat them while walking outside, letting the rhythm of my steps match the rhythm of my words. Regardless, the more often I practice, the stronger the foundation becomes. And that foundation makes it harder for life to shake me.

What interrupts your peace most often? Is it overcommitment? Overthinking? External drama? Recognize your triggers. You can't protect what you don't notice. What are three habits or boundaries you could implement to protect your mental clarity? Think small and specific. Maybe it's turning your phone off an hour earlier. Maybe it's saying no to one unnecessary meeting this week. Maybe it's a ten-minute morning walk without your phone in your hand. Protecting your peace doesn't always mean changing your life. Sometimes it means adjusting how you live it.

Describe your version of inner peace. What does it feel like? Look like? Maybe it's being fully present with your kids. Maybe it's working at a steady pace instead of sprinting. Maybe it's waking up without dread. Write it down. The more clearly you define what peace means to you, the easier it becomes to create it.

When I look back over the years, I see how much time I spent chasing things that didn't quiet my soul. I had moments of excitement, pride, and validation, but not the deep stillness that lasts.

Peace changes how we measure success. It makes us grateful instead of greedy. We still need to set goals, but now they'll serve our lives instead of consuming them. We still need to work hard, but now it'll be from rest instead of restlessness. That's the difference peace makes.

There will always be noise to contend with. The world won't stop demanding, competing, and comparing. But we don't have to join in to succeed. We can choose peace as our mental operating system, and build our wealth from a quiet mind instead of a frantic one.

The irony is, once we stop chasing everything, we start attracting the right things. Peace creates space for purpose to move in. So, protect it. Nurture it. Guard it as fiercely as you guard your time, your finances, or your reputation.

We can have money. We can have success. We can build a legacy. But peace helps to stitch each of these elements together into something cohesive instead of individual pieces.

The Invisibles: The Moments You Can't Measure

"Whoever can be trusted with very little can also be trusted with much..."
Luke 16:10

When people hear the word "wealth," their minds jump to salaries, investments, and assets. But as we've been discovering, real wealth isn't those things. Or at least not in isolation. Instead, one of the pillars of true wealth is found in the intangibles that give those things meaning.

The invisibles are the parts of life that don't show up on a balance sheet, but matter more than anything that does. They're not about accumulation, but appreciation. The warmth of the sun on your face during a walk, the sound of your child's laughter in another room, the quiet rhythm of your partner's breathing beside you at night, the peace that settles after a long workout or a deep prayer. These moments are the subtle, unadvertised forms of wealth that you only recognize when you slow down enough to feel them.

We spend so much time chasing *visible* success that we forget how much invisible value surrounds us. We wake up, check messages, rush to work, manage tasks, solve problems, and in the blur of motion, we stop seeing what matters most.

I used to do that daily. I'd walk past my family while thinking about business deals, or plan tomorrow's meetings while eating dinner, hardly tasting the food. I thought I was being productive, but I was actually being blind.

The invisibles don't vanish. They're still there, whether you notice them or not. But they lose their impact when we stop noticing them. And, even worse, when we stop noticing them, that trickles through our relationships, turning everything sour.

The Invisibles are what make life *feel* full, not just look full. When we hold someone's hand during a hard time. When we hear the ocean for the first time after a long year. When we laugh so hard, our stomachs hurt. Those experiences don't make us richer financially, but they do replenish us emotionally. And every time we pause to notice one, we're making a deposit into our inner account.

It's the same feeling we get after helping a friend without expecting anything in return. Or when someone remembers a small detail about us and brings it up later. That's the invisible exchange, the unspoken transfer of care, appreciation, or presence that keeps relationships alive.

We talked about compound interest earlier, and the same concept applies here. The more attention we give to the Invisibles, the more they multiply. Gratitude grows into joy. Joy turns into peace. Peace deepens connection. Connection strengthens meaning. And before long, you're living wealth daily instead of chasing numbers on a screen.

Defining the Invisibles

The Invisibles are the sensations, moments, and emotions that make life human. They're experiences you *feel.*

One of those Invisibles for me came from my granddaughter, Lily. Her school hosted a "bring a loved one to lunch" day, and she chose me. It was a small thing, but it carried weight because it showed how she sees me in her life. I was reminded that these quiet moments of being chosen, included, or remembered often matter more than objectively larger milestone celebrations. They're the ribbons that hold relationships together.

A few more examples are:

- The soft breeze at the beach that carries salt and memories.
- The look your partner gives you when words aren't needed.
- The quiet satisfaction after finishing a workout you didn't want to start.
- The first sip of coffee on a silent morning.

- The deep belly laugh that catches you off guard and reminds you that you're still alive.
- The stillness of early dawn before the world starts moving.
- The hug that lingers a second longer than expected.

Bart, with his wife Tina, and daughter, Tehani, in Moorea

Each of these is a form of wealth that can't be bought, and noticing makes our daily experiences feel like a life instead of a checklist of endless responsibilities and bids for our time and attention. Money pays for comfort, but the Invisibles create contentment. Without them, even abundance feels empty.

Think of people you've known who "had it all" but still seemed restless. They likely had the house, the car, the title, and yet, something was missing. They'd mastered earning but forgotten how to feel.

The Invisibles bring us back to that feeling and reconnect us to meaning. It's why the smallest moments can break through even the heaviest stress. They bypass logic and go straight to the soul. And the best part is, we don't need to earn them. We only need to *notice* them.

They're easy to talk about in theory, but the real power comes from living them; feeling them in moments so small, they seem ordinary until we notice how extraordinary they really are.

The Danger of Numbness

When life moves fast and everything becomes transactional, we lose our sensitivity to beauty. We stop noticing the subtle things because we're addicted to the next big, flashy thing. We chase intensity instead of intimacy, but intensity fades fast. The high of closing a deal or achieving a milestone lasts hours, maybe days, at most. But the satisfaction of invisible moments lingers and brings the emotions back to the surface each time they're noticed or remembered.

Neuroscience suggests our reward systems chase novelty, while experiences of bonding and calm are often associated with slower, steadier chemistry[5]. If we run our lives on the rises and drops of dopamine, and don't allow room for the gentle touch of oxytocin, we're setting ourselves up for a rollercoaster ride that'll never end. And sure, those highs feel great when they peak, but the lows that follow when the dopamine rush puts our sanity at risk can, in some cases, become genuinely life-threatening.

I've met people at the top of their industries who feel completely alone because their carefully crafted life lacks meaning. They chased the highs, then crashed into the lows and completely ignored the actual *life* part of living.

But climbing out of that pit of numbness doesn't need special tools, time, or training. We just need to slow down enough to notice the Invisibles. When you sit at the table with your family, put the phone away. Look people in the eye. Listen to their tone and watch their expressions. When you walk outside, take five seconds to feel the air on your skin. When you hug someone, hold them with both arms, and don't rush to let go. Over time, this practice will change your relationship with everything: your work, your health, your friends and family, and your goals.

---

[5] Costa, V. D., Tran, V. L., Turchi, J., & Averbeck, B. B. (2014). Dopamine modulates novelty seeking behavior during decision making. *Behavioral neuroscience*, *128*(5), 556–566. https://doi.org/10.1037/a0037128

Kids grow up. Parents age. Friends move away. Seasons change. And if we don't slow down now, one day, we'll look back and realize we traded priceless moments for things that no longer matter.

The Invisibles are generous. They don't hold grudges. So, the moment we begin noticing them, they start showing up again. Because they're actually always around, waiting for us to return to them.

A Different Kind of Wealth

So, what is invisible wealth, really? Well, it's not luck or luxury. It's just a state of awareness. It's being rich in appreciation, gratitude, and presence, and knowing that every day holds something worth remembering, even on the hard days.

The Invisibles don't replace material wealth, but they do help redefine it. They remind us that the goal of wealth isn't to own more, but to experience more deeply. Because what are we building financial wealth for? And who? Without a *reason* for the money, we might as well not even have it. And no, a new iPhone isn't the "reason." It's the excuse that keeps us from looking around and seeing where the real value is. But if we're making the money to be able to spend more time with our family, or to gift our parents the vacation of their dreams, that makes the effort worth it.

When we build a life that honors the Invisibles, we live better, mentally and emotionally, not just physically. It's for the freedom to be present. To sit still long enough to feel love, gratitude, and joy without needing to earn them. To know that peace isn't the result of what we're built, but the reward for finally slowing down to enjoy it.

The older I get, the more I realize that the things that truly matter can't be tallied or tracked. They're the moments that live quietly in memory. The small acts of love, laughter, and connection that make the rest of life worthwhile. They're presence. They're beauty. They're connection. They're feelings. And these aren't the metrics we measure, but they are the moments that *measure us*.

No financial statement can capture what it feels like to be hugged by our children, or cuddled by a pet, or to receive a simple text that says, "Thinking of you." Those things don't increase our net worth, but they do increase our sense of worth.

To reiterate from the relationships chapter, "someday" doesn't exist. "Someday, I'll take that trip." "Someday, I'll slow down." "Someday, I'll be more present." Someday is always waiting because it never arrives. Life doesn't pause to give us permission. It keeps moving. And the moments we think we can delay often don't repeat themselves.

Recently, my two grandchildren, Lily and Oliver, had their birthdays, and their single special request for their birthdays was to have time with me. We called it "Pop-pop time." So, I took time out of my usually busy schedule to specifically spend their special days with them. We went to the mall and did some shopping and slowed down for a day of one-on-one attention that can often feel challenging to experience when we're all so focused on our daily routines.

Moments like that teach us what money can't: how to feel alive. They remind us that the people who love us don't care about our title or achievements. They care about our presence. And that's something we can't outsource or postpone. Once we miss those moments, we can't buy them back.

There's a hidden cost to living for "later." We lose connection in real time. We miss birthdays, dinners, and unplanned laughter. We become visitors in our own lives, always nearby, but rarely actually *in them*.

Looking back, I see how many times I traded now for later. I told my kids, "We'll do that next weekend." I told my wife, "Let's plan a trip once things settle." I told myself, "I'll slow down once I reach this goal." And every time, life filled the space with new demands. Because there's always another project, or obligation, or reason to wait. But there's never another today.

The Invisibles strip away titles and achievements and leave only what's real: love, gratitude, and connection. We can say we value family, but do we prove it with our time? We can say we value presence, but do we give it without distraction?

Tying back to the Family & Friends pillar, when you're with your family, be with them. Consider it similar to when you taste a new wine for the first time: you want to swish the glass and take a small sip and savour it, really break down and identify the scent and flavours. We should treat time with our loved ones the same way. When you're walking outside, feel the gravel under your shoes. When you eat, taste the food. When you rest, let yourself *rest*. It sounds simple, but it's revolutionary in a world addicted to distraction.

Redefining Success

Success used to mean being needed by clients. Now, it also means being remembered by family. It used to mean having influence. Now, it means having an impact that starts at home. I still work hard. I still set goals. But now, I do it with the awareness that all of it means nothing if I'm too busy to enjoy what it supports.

The Invisibles fill that space. They remind us that a meaningful life isn't measured in accolades, but in affection. We don't need to retire to start enjoying life. We don't need to wait for a vacation or a milestone birthday. Peace and presence are available in the middle of the ordinary. So, the next time your child asks you to play, say yes. The next time your partner wants to talk, stop what you're doing and listen. The next time someone says, "I love you," let it land. The Invisibles aren't rare; they're everywhere. You just have to slow down long enough to truly experience them.

If something matters, it belongs on the calendar now, not in an undefined future. Because one day, "someday" turns into "too late." And when we reach that point, all the success in the world can't buy back what we missed.

We can find beauty in imperfection, joy in small gestures, and connection in quiet conversations. And the more we notice, the more abundant life feels.

When I think about what I want to leave behind, about that intentional legacy we talked about, I think about the memories and feelings created in the moment of the Invisibles. Because someday, my grandchildren won't remember what car I drove, or what projects I worked on. But they'll remember that I showed up, and was really mentally *with them.*

Reclaiming Invisible Wealth

Calm, presence, and attention: the three ingredients that unlock invisible wealth. Without them, even the most beautiful moments pass unnoticed. But with them, the simplest moments feel impactful.

The Invisibles aren't hiding from us. We're hiding from them by submerging ourselves in distraction after distraction, and turning everything into an emergency—when really, very few jobs actually put people at risk if we aren't running on overtime. The Invisibles don't need to be created. They're already there, waiting for you to slow down long enough to notice them.

Peace opens the door. Presence keeps it open.
Attention lets you walk through.

Peace gives you the stillness to notice. Presence grounds you in the moment. Attention turns the ordinary into the extraordinary.

We think we need new scenery or experiences to feel rich, but all we actually need is awareness. We can experience invisible wealth anywhere.

When we give someone our full attention, we give them presence. When we give it to ourselves, we give ourselves permission to live consciously and choose where our energy goes instead of letting the world decide for us. And when we direct that energy toward the Invisibles, life expands.

Instead of looking for how to make life slow down, look for how to slow *yourself* down. To notice it, you have to create space.

Here are a few simple ways to do that:

1. Turn off your phone during meals. Notice this one keeps popping up? There's a reason for that. There's something sacred about eating together without distractions. It's one of the few rituals that still brings people face to face. When you remove the constant buzz of notifications, you create room for genuine connection. The first few times I did this, it felt awkward, like something was missing. Now, the family rule is no phones at the table. It's a small thing that makes a big difference.
2. Sit outside with no agenda. We've forgotten how to be still without a "reason." We sit outside and immediately reach for

the next task (replying to messages, reading, checking the time). But when you sit without a plan, something changes. You start hearing things again. The wind through the trees. The sound of birds. Your own breathing. Stillness resets your nervous system and reminds you that life happens between your plans, not inside them. Even five minutes of quiet outside can reset an entire day.

3. Walk without headphones. Stop filling every moment with fabricated noise. No podcasts, calls, or music. Put it all away and just experience the world around you. The sound of your feet on the pavement. The rhythm of your breathing. The distant hum of life around you. That silence was more restorative than any playlist.
4. Watch the sunset without photographing it. We've trained ourselves to capture instead of experience. We see something beautiful, and our first instinct is to take out our phone. We want proof and a memory. But in doing so, we step out of the moment to preserve it. And the irony is, the photo rarely captures what the heart felt. Now, I leave the phone in my pocket when the sky turns gold. I let myself stand there and experience it first-hand.

The modern world is designed to steal presence and awareness from the minute we wake up to the moment we fall asleep. Our phones want our focus. Our work wants our time. Our thoughts want our attention. To reclaim presence, we have to practice it intentionally and anchor ourselves within our responsibilities. We can be present in a meeting, on a call, at dinner, in traffic—if we decide to show up fully.

Most people don't lack beauty or blessings in their lives. They lack the awareness to spot those things. They think fulfillment is hidden in something they haven't achieved yet, but invisible wealth it's right here. And it always has been. It's in our morning coffee, in the laughter that breaks tension, in the hug we didn't expect, in the simple relief of being alive. We've been taught to look past those things because they don't "look" like success, but they *feel* like success. And that's what matters.

The Art of Noticing

Noticing is a skill, and like all skills, it improves with practice. The more we notice beauty, the more we'll find it. The more we appreciate connection, the more it grows. Our brains are wired to lean into confirmation bias, so if we look for distractions, or look for reasons to feel taken advantage of by the world, we'll "find" exactly those things. But if we start looking for the good things in life, we'll see just how many Invisibles are right in front of us, every hour of every day.

It's like tuning a radio. At first, the signal crackles, but once we find the right frequency, the sound becomes clear. The frequency of invisible wealth is gratitude. The static is a distraction. But every time we pause, breathe, and notice, we're tuning ourselves to experience gratitude.

Some of the most meaningful moments are deceptively simple. Sitting quietly with my wife Tina, no words needed. Hearing Christian or Nicole's voice on the phone. Watching Tehani chase waves at the beach. Those moments don't announce themselves. They arrive quietly, and if we're not paying attention, they pass unnoticed. That's why our attention is sacred. It's how we honor the moment we're in.

Building invisible wealth comes down to reworking old habits into new ones. Eat slower. Listen longer. Speak softer. Breathe deeper. Give yourself permission to enjoy small things without guilt. And when you catch yourself trying to multitask or document every experience, pause and ask yourself, "What if I just lived this instead?"

We've become obsessed with "proof." We want evidence for every good thing ("pics or it didn't happen"). But the most meaningful parts of life don't leave evidence. No one can photograph peace. We can't post presence. We can't quantify love. The Invisibles are meant to be felt, not shared (except by the people in that moment with us). When we stop needing to prove our joy to the world, we start experiencing it fully.

My Favorite Invisibles

The things I treasure most aren't the ones I can show off or count. They're the ones that live quietly in my memory: the sights, sounds, and sensations that ground me. They're small, fleeting, and easy to miss, but when I pay attention, they're everywhere.

Here are some of my favorite invisibles:

A wave breaking the sunrise. There's something humbling about that moment. The way the horizon glows just before the sun appears, how the sound of the surf syncs with my breathing. It's like the world reminding me to start again. Every sunrise is proof that no matter what happened yesterday, today is another chance.

The warmth of a towel after a swim. It's such a simple pleasure. The kind of comfort that feels earned. The cold fades, my muscles relax, and for a moment, everything feels balanced.

Eye contact during a real conversation. Undivided attention is one of the rarest gifts we can give in our modern age of endless distractions and limitless comparisons splashed across our phones.

Affection and gratitude from and with my loved ones. While reading through one of the early drafts of this book, I lay on the couch, flipping through a printed copy, when Tehani (now ten years old) walked into the room. She asked what I was up to, so I showed her the Foreword and Acknowledgements sections. After reading it, she hugged me, tears streaming down her face, and said, "I love you." These kind of unfiltered and freely given connections can't be replicated in any other way. It's how our hearts reach out to one another, extending beyond the bounds of our physical bodies.

The moment I feel like myself again. We all lose touch with ourselves sometimes. Life gets loud. Stress builds. We become a version of ourselves that we don't quite recognize. Then, one day, we take a deep breath, smile without effort, and realize we're home again. That moment is invisible wealth in its purest form; the quiet return to who we are beneath all the chaos.

An amazing glass of wine along with deep conversation. We need reminders to slow down and not only remove ourselves from the hustle and bustle of the world, but also take time to appreciate the people we have in our lives. By connecting with them on a deeper level than the typical surface discussions we engage in while we're endlessly busy, I can experience the fullness of who they are.

When we start writing down the small moments that bring us peace or joy, we begin to see patterns, and most of them don't involve money. They don't require travel, achievement, or planning, either. They just require awareness.

Grab a notebook or open a blank note on your phone and start your own list. Don't overthink it. Just write what comes to mind. Here are some more ideas:

- The sound of rain against the window.
- The smell of coffee before the first sip.
- The way your pet greets you at the door.
- The calm after a workout.
- The laughter of someone you love.

- The feeling of finishing a hard day, knowing you gave it your best.
- The softness of clean sheets.
- The relief of forgiveness.
- The stillness of early morning, when the world hasn't started moving yet.

Once you start your list, add to it often. Keep it nearby so you can reread it when you feel anxious, rushed, or disconnected. It's not a bucket list, but a grounding list; a collection of moments that bring you back to the present.

When we train our minds to notice the Invisibles, life stops passing by unnoticed. We can feel things more deeply, and connect more honestly, bringing more value to moments for what they mean, not what they produce.

It's easy to think gratitude is about being thankful for what we have. And we *should* be grateful for and aware of what we have. But invisible wealth goes further, into being grateful for what we *feel*.

They're personal, unrepeatable, and timeless. They're not meant to impress anyone. They're meant to nourish us. And life starts meaning more when we stop trying to measure everything,

If you want to experience invisible wealth daily, slow down enough to let the moment catch up with you. That might mean leaving your phone in another room for an hour, or sitting outside at dusk and watching the light change, or walking somewhere you've driven a hundred times before, just to see what you've been missing. Or perhaps it means asking someone how they're doing and actually listening to the answer. None of these require effort or expense. They just require the willingness to be in the now.

What invisible moments brought you joy in the past week? Was it a conversation? A sound? A look? A feeling? Revisit it in your mind. Relive it for a few seconds. You'll be surprised how much peace you can draw from a single remembered moment.

What habits keep you too distracted to notice them? Is it constant scrolling? Overcommitment? Multitasking? Awareness is the first step toward change. Identify what pulls your attention away from the present and decide how to reclaim it.

Create your own list. Aim for ten items. Start simple. Keep it personal and add to it often. You'll notice how quickly your perception changes.

The Invisibles are always present. We just lose sight of them when we move too fast or look too far ahead. But they're patient. The moment we return to awareness, they welcome us back. And when we start seeing invisible wealth for what it is, we realize we've been rich all along.

Real wealth isn't something we can display. It's something we can feel. And the more we pay attention, the more abundant life becomes.

Finance: The Tool, Not the Goal

"Godliness with contentment is great gain... we brought nothing into the world, and we can take nothing out of it."
1 Timothy 6:6–7

And finally, here it is. Finance *is* a form of wealth, but finance comes last for a reason.

My first real paycheck gave me a sense of pride, but it didn't make me feel fulfilled. And this is a pattern we see all the time. There are people with millions who are miserable (and end up splashed across the covers of tabloids when their unhappiness causes them to crash out), while some other, more modest people might sleep like kings, despite their financial security being a daily struggle. The contrast proves that money doesn't guarantee meaning. It solves problems, yes. It provides freedom. But it doesn't create peace, love, or joy.

When money is in its right place, it supports our lives. But when it's not, it runs our lives. And the only way to understand that balance is to experience both sides of it, because it's scarcity that shapes our habits, and abundance that tests our character.

As we've already covered, I didn't grow up around wealth. We were considered low/middle-class. There were months when the bills stacked higher than the paychecks, even with my mother working side jobs and my father's steady employment as a truck driver. And vacations weren't a thing. Eating out was rare. New clothes often came from discount racks and off-brand labels, and even then, they had to last a long time. My mother would sew patches into our pants whenever our jeans tore, and by the end of every school year, the hems were too short, since we weren't able to constantly buy new clothes to keep up with my growth. But there was a kind of pride in making it work.

Despite their challenges, my parents were resourceful in ways that only people who've struggled know how to be. My mom could stretch a grocery budget as if it were a competitive sport. She knew every sale and every shortcut to make something out of nothing. Which is how, despite not being financially secure throughout my childhood, by the time I was old enough to get my first car, my mother was able to loan me half the cost for it in cash using money she'd saved from years of odd jobs like babysitting the neighbours and Tupperware sales.

When we talked about legacy, I mentioned the $20,000 we found tucked away in little envelopes and under the mattress once she passed away. In today's economy, that's not even enough to live off for a year, but her resourcefulness did exactly what it was supposed to do. And while I can't know for certain, it's my impression that it gave her a sense of control and power, despite us living a life that didn't offer us much of those things otherwise.

I started working early. Before fifteen, I moved lawns, and I collected used newspapers and recycled them for money. And one summer, I worked at a skateboard shop assembling boards to earn my own money and build a sense of ownership. It wasn't glamorous work, but it built habits.

When I was fifteen and a half, I got a job at a fish and chips shop, the kind of place where you came home smelling like oil and salt for days. The hours were long, and the pay was low, but it gave me independence. And the first time I cashed a paycheck, it felt like freedom in my hands. It wasn't much, but it was mine. And I learned through working young that I didn't have to depend on someone else for my survival (or my sense of worth).

Money is merely a vehicle that allows us to make choices. And it's that freedom to make choices that actually garners happiness, not the money that enables those choices.

Scarcity has a way of teaching lessons that abundance can't. When you don't have much, you learn to appreciate what's in front of you, value effort over entitlement, respect the cost of things, and think twice before wasting time or money. You become intentional, whether you realize it or not, and every decision carries weight because you know the price of mistakes. And that pressure shapes you. It sharpens your instincts and your empathy.

It's why so many people who grow up with very little become incredible leaders later in life, because they're so intimately familiar with what it takes to live at the ground level. They don't look down on hard work because they don't forget the struggle. They know what it means to go without, and that memory keeps them grounded, even when they finally reach success.

Why Money Comes Last

That's why finance comes last in this framework of True Wealth, because until we understand health, relationships, faith, service, legacy, peace, and the Invisibles, money doesn't mean much. What would you even do with more money if you don't have and don't value the other pillars of wealth?

It's easy to accidentally idolize the idea of net worth. But what we often don't see is how, without the other pillars of wealth keeping our net worth grounded, no amount of money will ever be "enough." Which is why many people lost track of the important things in life; they unintentionally became too fixated on finances alone.

As I mentioned in the first chapter, without the other forms of wealth, financial success becomes hollow. It gives us comfort, but not fulfillment. Money is a tool, not a trophy. It's meant to serve our values instead of replacing them, so when we allow money to become our master, it controls our decisions, relationships, and even our sense of self-worth. But when we treat it as a servant and a tool, it amplifies what we already have.

If you're generous, money allows us to give more. If we're fearful, money fuels that fear. If we're content, money gives us freedom. If we're restless, money becomes a distraction.

Consider how Steve Rogers became Captain America. The super-soldier serum they injected him with made him physically strong, but it was designed to enhance the elements someone already had inside them. So, Steve Rogers became the noble, heroic Captain America because his heart and mind kept his newfound strengths in check. But when the serum was eventually used on other people, the results were completely different. Or rather, the serum brought out those people's strongest traits, which were often not the same kind of traits Steve Rogers based his moral compass on.

Money is like the super-soldier serum. It doesn't change us. But it does reveal who we really are and what we value (or rather, where we lack in values).

Even today, when I see financial success, I remember that small house where my mom hid bills in envelopes. I remember the smell of fish and oil from my first job, and the growl of the Volkswagen I bought with her help, and the pride that came from developing my own sense of self and ownership instead of being handed luxury. And it's those memories that keep me grounded.

Money can't buy contentment. Contentment comes from alignment and living by our values instead of by our valuables.

The Real Currency

At its core, money is energy. It moves, circulates, grows, and shrinks depending on how we treat it. When we hoard it, it stagnates. When we use it with intention, it multiplies (and not just financially, but emotionally and spiritually, too). Because every financial decision is also a values decision.

What we spend on shows what we prioritize. What we give toward shows what we believe in. What we save for shows what we hope for.

Money itself is neutral. It's what we attach to it that gives it meaning. Money can support our fulfillment and make it easier for us to make decisions that deepen our faith, peace, love, and purpose, and earn us more time. But money can't inherently provide us with that fulfillment on its own.

Two people can earn the same income and live in entirely different emotional states. One might feel grounded, generous, and aligned with personal values. The other person might feel pressured, become defensive, and consumed by fear of losing what they've built. The difference isn't the money. It's the meaning assigned to it and the behavior that meaning creates.

When money functions as a tool instead of a scoreboard, it frees us rather than binding us. It gives us room to protect our health, time, and relationships. It allows space for education, travel, or recovery during demanding seasons. But it also reveals patterns that need attention. Overspending often points to stress or avoidance. Underspending often points to fear or scarcity.

Money also teaches discipline. Planning ahead, delaying gratification, and separating needs from desires strengthen traits that influence every other pillar. And these habits spill into how we parent, how we lead teams, and how we show up in our communities. Financial steadiness reduces emotional chaos, bringing a level of contentment that makes purpose-driven work easier to sustain.

Responsibility Before Wealth

I wasn't taught about investing or credit or building wealth. Those concepts didn't exist in my house growing up. There were no lessons on compound interest or asset allocation. The focus was on survival. If we could cover bills in time and have a little left over, that was success.

When I was still quite young, my father bought his own freight truck, believing he would be able to make more money that way instead of relying on the trucks provided by the company he hauled for. It didn't work out the way he expected, and although I don't know the details as to why it failed, we eventually ended up staying with friends of the family for a few weeks. I only later learned that it was because he was trying to dodge his truck getting repossessed.

Ultimately, his truck was found and did get repossessed. But despite the confusion during that situation, I still took a lesson away from it. Not all our risks pan out. And we need to have the foresight to know what the consequences will be if our idea fails, and we need to be willing to accept the chance of facing those consequences.

But of course, it took time for that lesson, among others, to really sink into me as I got older. So, when I stepped out into the world, I had to learn everything the hard way.

No one told me how debt worked, or what a healthy financial plan looked like. I made mistakes, but I figured things out through trial and error and curiosity. What I lacked in knowledge, I made up for with a hunger to understand.

When I was accepted to the University of California, San Diego, it felt like a dream. It was validation that all the long hours, good grades, side jobs, and study sessions had been worth it. But I was also confronted head-on with my own emotional immaturity.

I wasn't ready.

To attend UC San Diego, I would've had to apply for financial aid. And the idea of taking on debt and diving into a huge, unfamiliar environment felt overwhelming. I couldn't articulate it at the time, but something in me knew I wasn't equipped to handle it.

So, I enrolled at Orange Coast Community College instead. It gave me time to mature, figure out who I was, and learn at my own pace. A part of me worried I'd failed by not taking the "big leap," but looking back, it was one of my first real financial decisions, and it taught me that "more expensive" doesn't necessarily mean better. I later finished my education at Cal State University, Fullerton.

Like most first-generation students, I worked my way through school. I had classes in the morning and shifts in the afternoon, then tumbled into study sessions at night. Which taught me that time is also a currency, or rather, a finite asset. If you don't manage your time well, you'll run out of it just the same as any other kind of currency. Money was always tight. Rent, gas, food; it all had to be earned week to week. But those years strengthened and built on the foundational work ethic that started back at home.

While other students were figuring out where to party, I was figuring out how to balance my budget. I didn't have the luxury of drifting. Every hour mattered. And it was through that grind that I developed a respect for the value of effort.

And then, in the middle of my college career, my then-girlfriend became pregnant, which added another layer to my already multi-layered situation. I now also had a young wife (we got married while she was pregnant) and a newborn baby to care for, on top of finishing college and working.

Most people my age (I was twenty-two when Nicole was born) were still figuring themselves out. Meanwhile, I was figuring out how to provide for someone else. For *two* someone elses. And it changed everything. Money wasn't just about me anymore. It wasn't about cars or clothes or convenience, either. It was about diapers, baby food, and the tiny human who depended on me to keep the lights on.

The responsibility was heavy, but it forced me to grow up fast. I learned to plan, save, and think long-term before I even knew what long-term truly meant. Those early years were lean. There were times when we had to make tough choices about which bills to pay when and which we could "let" slide for a little longer. And the financial strain didn't get easier as my then-wife slowly became an addict. But those challenges taught me that financial success is about how we manage the money we make, not how *much* money we make. Even millionaires can go broke if they mismanage their spending. And the act of managing money well is an act of love (self-love and love for the people who rely on you).

From Computers to People

I worked for ABBA Computers when my son Christian was born. I loved it there, with the mix of business, hardware, and software focus. My job required me to make cold calls, then meet with the companies in-person. And it was through that change in my career that I managed to secure our finances and meet all my financial goals by the age of thirty.

And yet, it wasn't *truly* fulfilling. Perhaps the challenges I faced in my personal life played a role in how I felt at the time too, considering my marriage had long-before stopped being a healthy situation. But the moment that made me evaluate if this was what I wanted to keep doing for the rest of my life was when I landed the biggest sale the company had ever had. The company couldn't handle the scope of the project, and what should have been the best opportunity ended up sinking the business instead, and they had to let me go.

That situation is the perfect example of the value of the *amount* of something being dependent on our capacity to manage it.

The turning point came during a casual conversation with my financial advisor. I spoke with him about my desire to change other people's lives and make a bigger impact on other people's success and freedom. I was already in my thirties and professionally doing well for myself, but I hadn't yet felt fulfilled in what I'd been doing, despite my accomplishments up to that point. He said that his occupation as a financial advisor was changing people's lives and suggested coming to work for his company.

If you remember from the beginning of the book, I thought about it for months before making a decision. Until one day, I woke up in the middle of the night with a firm sense of what can only be described as my "aha" moment, and decided to finally do it. I had to get a securities and insurance license by night while still holding a computer sales job during the day, and it took nine months to become fully ready to step into the role of a financial advisor. And even once I had the credentials, I had to compensate for the initial financial loss by picking up a side job as a bouncer at a bar and doing some modeling while building up my client base. But helping people make smarter financial decisions combined everything I cared about: education, relationships, and long-term development.

Bart modelling for Trouble in LA, a division of LA Models

I ended up staying with the firm for twenty-five years, and I was able to build my own practice under the umbrella name of the company.

I even eventually recruited my brother to manage the medical insurance side of the business. But in 2016, I felt it was time to make another change to better serve my clients, and I joined another firm.

This company asked me to join them and take over the company within a few years, as the owner planned to retire. It meant taking my clients with me to the new company. But I put in the work, and the first year went smoothly. It was when the buyout process started (sooner than expected) that things got messy.

The plans had changed; it would be a joint sale along with another person who'd been a part of the company for longer than me. And when I walked into the meeting with her, which was supposed to solidify her gaining 40% and me gaining 60%, she announced that she bought 100% of the company the night before. The previous owner said his hands were tied because she was already part owner with him. And her first act as the full solo owner was firing my assistant.

It was a terrible situation. Especially considering that, at that time, I'd recently experienced the birth of Tehani after remarrying and eight years of trying to start a family with Tina. But it allowed me the freedom to move on to other things, despite the stressful and unforeseen circumstances. I stayed there for another nine months while looking for a new Registered Investment Advisory (RIA) to align with and planning to start my own company.

I firmly believe things happen for a reason and that God has bigger plans for us. So, as rough as that situation was, and as hurt as I was, it was the best thing for me in the long run. And today, I run a very successful business, which proves that the pain I felt during the breakup of the previous financial company was all for a good reason.

Looking back, none of those career moves were random. Each one exposed the difference between financial success and personal alignment. I earned well and advanced quickly. I hit milestones that looked impressive from the outside. Yet fulfillment lagged behind achievement, and security proved fragile when it depended solely on income or position. The failed sale, the corporate politics, the shifting ownership agreements, and the unexpected job losses all reinforced the lesson that money, titles, and opportunity only hold value if they align with purpose and integrity.

Capacity matters more than scale. A career isn't meant to define a life; it's meant to support one.

What Money Means Now

Through all these ups and downs in my career path, it wasn't that I had a certain amount of money that mattered. It was that I had just enough financial resources to have the *freedom* to keep looking for where I fit in best and what worked for me and my professional (and personal) needs. In my youth, I didn't have the time or money to make the kinds of choices I can make now. And it has very little to do with age.

When people at the top look at people at the bottom and say, "Just get a better job then," they completely miss the point. The people at the bottom literally *can't* find a "better" job because they don't have the freedom afforded to them to do that. They don't have the financial security as a foundation to build on. And it's the people who struggle on the ground who end up getting taken advantage of by the people above them, making their time "currency" even tighter as well.

Without the other elements of True Wealth, making money can lead either to reckless and pointless spending in a desperate search for the happiness that's missing, or hoarding what we earn out of fear of it being taken from us. We need the other pillars first and foremost, but we also need to be able to financially support ourselves and our loved ones. Money matters. Our worldwide economy demands the earning and spending of it. But having money without purpose is far lonelier and more mentally devastating than being rich in all the other kinds of wealth.

Only once we have those other pillars of wealth does earning money truly give us the freedom to choose how we spend our time and who we spend it with, the impact to support the causes and people we care about, and the legacy to create stability for our children and teach them what real wealth looks like.

When I think about that kid who didn't know what credit was or how interest worked, I'm grateful for him. He learned by doing. He stumbled, failed, and figured it out piece by piece. And every mistake became a lesson. Every small win built confidence. And those lessons shaped not just my career, but also my philosophy that money is meant to serve us instead of ruling us.

From my perspective, the goal isn't to only have more. It's to live better with what we have while teaching others to do the same. That's what drives me now.

When I talk to clients today, I see reflections of who I used to be; people who are doing their best with the knowledge they have. And it's my role to remind them that financial wisdom is *learned.* And anyone *can* learn it. You don't need a degree in economics. You just need curiosity, consistency, and a willingness to face uncomfortable truths. Because money, at its core, is simple. It's not about luck or intelligence. Whether we are "rich" all comes down to our mentality and behavior. And once we learn to manage that, we realize we don't have to chase wealth. We can instead build it, slowly and sustainably, in service of something bigger than ourselves.

That's the difference between living for money and letting money serve your life.

Good Enough

Consider how different our lives would feel if more people were taught the value of having "enough," and how to balance it with the other elements of True Wealth. Enough to live without fear. Enough to choose our schedule. Enough to give freely and sleep peacefully. Chasing more is an endless energy drain with no end-goal. There's no stopping point, no end of the race. We just keep running, and running, and running until we can't anymore and collapse. But if we have a goal, a metric of "enough" to ensure we always have healthy food on the table, a roof over our heads and a bed to sleep in, clean clothes on our bodies, and just enough extra to have some casual comforts in life, that sustains us.

This concept is the basis for the universal basic income experiments, which provided all adult citizens with regular government payments, regardless of their financial or employment status, to alleviate poverty and support their basic needs. The premise was to ensure every household receives exactly "enough" to cover rent, simple groceries, and self-care products (like toilet paper). And for everything else someone wanted in their life, all the comforts and luxuries that go beyond the basic needs, they had to work to earn more money to cover those additional things. These experiments inherently teach the idea of "enough," and encourage people to put in effort toward designing their standard of "enough" beyond the essentials.

Of course, this isn't fail-proof. Some people might determine they "need" to be a billionaire to be making "enough" money, but when we're grounded in the other pillars as well, it's unlikely for anyone to feel this way. Because alignment with the other pillars of True Wealth changes our perception from "time is money" to "what is enough to convert into time with my family, health for my body, services to those around me, faith and self-development, peace of mind, enjoying the invisibles, and building something to leave behind?"

The Four Cornerstones of Financial Freedom

When I think about what financial success really means, it always comes back to four things:

1. Security

Financial security is about stability. Knowing that if something goes wrong (a job loss, a medical bill, an unexpected emergency), we're covered. The size of our income alone doesn't matter without our health, for example. What matters is the strength of our safety net. It's the peace that comes from knowing we've built a foundation solid enough to weather storms.

2. Flexibility

True Wealth gives us options. It lets us change directions when life changes without feeling trapped by obligations or debt. Flexibility means we can take a break, switch careers, help a loved one, or move somewhere new without financial panic. And that freedom to make choices based on values instead of fear is one of life's greatest luxuries.

3. Control Over Time

Money buys time, but only if we use it wisely. When we manage our finances intentionally, we gain control over how we spend our days. We're no longer chained to every opportunity out of necessity, and we start making decisions from desire instead of being controlled by desperation.

4. Peace of Mind

This is the ultimate goal: the confidence that your financial life aligns with your values and supports your purpose. Peace of mind comes from knowing your money serves your life, not the other way around.

The Trap of "More"

The pursuit of "more" is based in comparison. And that's how money becomes our master. Companies know this, too. Which is why when one new innovative product or company hits the market, there's always a rush of competing companies suddenly flooding the scene, all trying to get our attention. They self-fuel the idea that they're competing and make us, the consumers, feel like we're competing with each other based on which company we've given our money to.

Apple doesn't *need* to release a new iPhone model every year. They do it to make us feel like we need whatever new features and hardware they've put into it. They create this concept of "need more" not only by competing with other phone brands, but also by making us compete with our past decisions. Our old phone, which isn't even old, is no longer "good enough." So even though we know they'll just keep releasing a new model year after year, making our current device no longer desirable, we keep playing the game.

We keep running. And we keep buying.

But once we actually understand what it really means to have "enough," and what we actually need to achieve that goal, everything changes. Our self-worth isn't tied to our net worth anymore, or how much we can spend and how quickly.

When money becomes a substitute for meaning, you'll always feel short on both.

But the path to "enough" requires us to pause and look at our lives and form healthy, consistent, intentional habits through our choices over time. Here are a few that have changed my life, and the lives of my clients:

1. Budgeting With Purpose

Most people think of budgeting as a punishment, as some kind of reminder of what they can't spend. But a real budget isn't restrictive. It shows where your values show up in your bank account, and when handled right, budgeting becomes a statement of priorities.

If family time matters, distribute resources for experiences together. If peace matters, simplify your subscriptions, automate your bills, and remove financial clutter. Make your budget purposeful and align with what you value.

2. Avoiding Lifestyle Inflation

Lifestyle inflation is one of the biggest traps of financial growth. You earn more, so you spend more, and this slowly turns into entitlement. But the problem isn't the spending itself. Unconscious spending is the true enemy.

Every upgrade feels justified in the moment, but over time, it locks you into dependency. You start needing more to feel satisfied. The key is awareness. Each time your income increases, resist the urge to expand your lifestyle. Expand your freedom instead.

3. Build an Emergency Fund

Life doesn't give warnings. Cars break down. Jobs disappear, and health changes overnight. Having three to six months of expenses set aside as a security net means there's no reason to worry about these eventualities crashing down on you. And when something happens that's unexpected, you can handle it without fearing if you can still afford your necessities this month.

4. Automate Savings and Investments

When you automate, you remove emotion from the process, which helps you prioritize saving before you can spend and invest without the risk of indulgence. And even small amounts add up over time.

Don't worry, I'm not telling you that if you just stop having that daily latte, you'll become rich. Instead, automating means you won't accidentally spend money that's going to be needed to cover a surprise bill coming next week, which allows you to look at your account and determine if you can afford to still treat yourself.

5. Work With an Advisor

You can't see every blind spot on your own, and a good financial advisor can help you manage your mindset in addition to managing your money. They challenge assumptions, protecting against impulsive decisions, and hold you accountable to your goals.

6. Teach Your Kids Early

Money habits start young. If you don't teach your kids about money, someone else will—and that someone probably wants to sell them something.

Teach them that money is a tool, and show them what generosity looks like. Involve them in small decisions. Let them earn, save, and give from an early age. You can't guarantee your children's future wealth, but you can shape their financial wisdom.

Full Circle

If there's one thing the journey through every pillar of wealth has taught me, it's that money was never the ultimate measure of success. It was merely the byproduct of something deeper. Each element—health, family and friends, faith, service, legacy, peace, and the invisibles—revealed a truth about perseverance that money alone could never teach.

Health taught me endurance. Family taught me loyalty. My Faith taught me trust. Service taught me generosity. Legacy taught me responsibility. Peace taught me contentment. The Invisibles taught me awareness. And together, they built a foundation that money could never replace.

There's always another benchmark. Another client. Another deal. Another "someday." We never truly arrive. We only learn how to keep walking without losing ourselves along the way. That's what perseverance is: moving forward with purpose.

But no amount of money could fix the terrible experiences from my first marriage. Or give me back time with my eldest children that I missed out on while trying to keep up with the system and support them. The more I earned, the more my worries evolved, because the problems were *still there*.

Contentment and fulfilment doesn't come from having enough money. It comes from knowing what enough means for you. And once you reach it, using it properly.

We like to think money is logical. But money is emotional. It reflects fear, pride, hope, guilt, and identity. It reveals how we were raised, what we value, and where we seek validation. Money is behavioral before it's mathematical. If it were purely logical, everyone would save more, spend less, and plan perfectly. But humans don't naturally operate like that.

We don't manage money. We manage emotions, and our emotions manage our money. We can know how to budget and still overspend. We can know how to invest and still panic-sell. We can know the importance of saving and still avoid opening our bank app.

Our brains weren't built for modern money. We're wired for survival instead of long-term planning. So, when we face a financial decision, the emotional brain reacts before the rational brain ever gets a chance.

1. Scarcity Mode: Why Stress Makes Us Spend or Freeze

Growing up with scarcity teaches you powerful lessons, but it also creates emotional reflexes: you hold on to money even when it's wise to invest. You spend impulsively when you finally get "extra," because it feels like relief. You avoid talking about money because it triggers old stress. Scarcity teaches discipline, but it can also teach fear. And fear quietly becomes a financial strategy unless you name it.

2. Comparison Mode: Why We Overspend Without Realizing It

One of the most dangerous financial traps is comparison. People don't necessarily go broke because they're irresponsible. They go broke because they're trying to keep up with a lifestyle that was never theirs to begin with. Every scroll, every feed, every "success story" creates a silent pressure that whispers, "You're behind." "You're not enough yet." "You should be doing more."

3. Reward Mode: Why "I Deserve It" Can Be a Trap

After long days, long weeks, or long seasons of stress, small luxuries feel earned, and sometimes they are. But the struggle comes when "deserving" becomes the explanation for every impulse. "I deserve it" is often code for, "I'm overwhelmed." It's an emotional response dressed up as a financial decision.

4. Avoidance Mode: Why We Look Away from Hard Numbers

People avoid opening statements or checking bank balances purely because they're anxious. Avoidance is a coping mechanism that gives temporary relief, but it also creates long-term damage. And avoiding numbers never avoids the consequences.

5. Identity Mode: How Your Financial Story Creates Your Financial Behavior

Whether you grew up with scarcity, instability, comfort, or chaos, you developed a personal money story. "I have to handle everything alone." "I'm bad with money." "I need to save every dollar." "Money always disappears." "I never have enough." These stories become scripts, and scripts become habits. But the moment you question the scripts, you can create the possibility of a new direction.

Recognize what triggers you. Understand your patterns. Notice where you overreact or underreact. Learn how your past shapes your present, and name the fears behind your decisions.

Money reflects us. It reveals our fears, our hopes, our habits, our self-worth. And the more aware we become, the more aligned our financial decisions become with the lives we want to live.

We operate on stories. The story of what money meant growing up. The story of what success is supposed to look like. The story of what will finally make us feel safe. And those stories run deeper than most people realize, which is why true financial mastery begins with emotional intelligence.

It's not enough to know what to do. You have to understand why you do what you do. Emotional intelligence in money means understanding your triggers, patterns, and beliefs before they control your behavior. Ask yourself, do you spend to feel secure or to feel seen? Do you save out of wisdom or out of fear? Do you equate net worth with self-worth?

Once you start noticing those patterns, you gain power over them and can stop reacting emotionally to money. Using money intentionally turns it from a source of anxiety into a source of awareness, and you begin to see that every financial decision is also a reflection of your values.

Over time, I've noticed that people who feel genuinely wealthy (not necessarily rich but fulfilled) share a few common behaviors. They plan without the control of obsession. They save without worry about also giving to others. They spend, but they do it with intention. They frequently live below their means instead of beneath their joy. They view money as a tool to create better relationships instead of replacing them. They talk openly about finances with their partners and children to educate them on the value of "enough." And most importantly, they don't make money their personality. They treat it as one part of a much larger equation; an amplifier for a life that already has meaning.

The idea of financial freedom used to mean never worrying about money again. Now, I define it as the ability to make decisions without fear or guilt. It's being able to say yes to what aligns with our values and no to what doesn't. We can't eliminate struggle from our lives, but we can use money to prepare ourselves to handle any challenges that come our way. We can't escape our responsibilities, but we can take ownership and make choices about how we want that ownership to function. We need to learn to appreciate what we have and when we have "enough."

Take a few minutes to reflect on where you stand in your relationship with money. What did you learn about money growing up? How is it helping or hindering you now? What does financial freedom look like to you? Does it mean no debt? More travel? Working less? Giving more? What financial habit can you commit to today to move toward true wealth?

Money will always be in motion. It's designed to move. But if we learn to let it serve us rather than allowing it to steer our decisions, it becomes a vehicle for everything that matters most.

True Wealth in Action, Living the Life You've Built

"Honor your body, love your people, build a legacy, trust deeply, give freely, live in peace, act with integrity, and keep money in its proper place."

I've carried one vision for years. In fact, I told you about my Statement of Vision earlier: *On my ninetieth birthday, I walk a mile on the beach in front of my home, hand-in-hand with my wife. Friends and family await us so we can enjoy cake together.* And that image sums up everything we've talked about. It's a snapshot of True Wealth in action. Because that single moment—being on the beach, surrounded by people I love—only exists if every pillar of my life remains strong.

When I think about that Statement of Vision we talked about earlier, I see more than a celebration. I see a lifetime of small, intentional choices.

Health is the ability to walk that mile. It's every morning I woke up early to exercise. Every time I skipped the easy option and chose to move, stretch, and stay consistent. It's knowing that strength isn't built in one moment, but protected every day. If I don't take care of my body now, that beach won't be part of my future.

Family and Friends are the people waiting when I arrive. The laughter, the hugs, the shared stories; that's what makes the moment complete. It means I stayed connected. I showed up for birthdays, games, dinners, and calls even when life was busy. I said, "I love you," more than, "I'll get to it later." Because when we nurture our relationships, we never have to wonder who'll be there when we need them most. And Tina holding my hand says that she still likes me after all these years!

Faith in God is the quiet belief that I'll live long enough to see that day. It's the unseen foundation beneath every goal. Faith gives meaning to effort and keeps me grounded when progress feels slow. And my Faith reminds me that every day I'm given is another chance to align my actions with my purpose.

Service is reflected in the way I've spent those years leading up to that beach day, focused on who I've helped through my achievements. It's the volunteer work, the mentorship, the quiet acts of generosity that will continue to impact other people's lives long after I'm gone. When I look around at that celebration, I don't want to see people who admire what I've built. I want to see people whose lives are better because I gave something back.

Legacy is the generations gathered: kids, grandkids, and friends who became family. It's about who continues the values I lived by, and it's knowing that I've taught my children and their children not only how to make a living, but also how to live meaningfully.

Peace is the contentment of that moment, the calm that comes from knowing I lived aligned with my values. It's not the absence of struggle, but instead the presence of gratitude. Peace means I can look around that beach, feel the breeze, hear the waves, and know that I've done my best with the time I had.

The Invisibles are in everything I can't photograph. The sunlight warming my face. The laughter of my wife. The salt in the air. The feeling of complete presence. Those moments are small, but sacred. They don't cost a thing, but they define everything.

Finance is what allows that day to be enjoyed freely with no stress, no constraints, and no distractions. Financial health is what lets me focus on people instead of problems, and makes space for gratitude, having the wherewithal to afford that home on the beach.

When I see that vision in my mind, I know that every pillar is holding it up. If I remove one, just one of the pillars of True Wealth, the whole picture changes.

Take a moment and picture the life you say you want. Not the résumé version, but the lived version. What does an ordinary Tuesday look like? Who's there? How does your body feel? What pace are you moving at? What fills your calendar?

Now, hold that vision steady and ask yourself: which of the eight pillars are supporting it? And what happens to that picture if your health weakens? Or your relationships strain? Or your peace disappears? Or your finances dominate everything else?

Which pillar feels strong right now? Which one feels unstable? And if one were removed entirely, how different would your vision look?

Why There's No Finish Line

People often ask when they'll "arrive." When they'll finally feel successful, stable, and content. But there is no finish line. There never has been, regardless of what the top one percent have claimed.

We don't graduate from health. We don't finish relationships. We don't master faith or peace once and for all. True wealth is a discipline practiced daily through choices, habits, and priorities.

And every pillar requires our attention. When one weakens, the others feel it. It's like balance; you don't find it once. You keep adjusting to maintain it.

By society's standards, as well as my own, I'm relatively successful. But as I've revealed, there've been times in my life when business took over and my connection with my family slipped. Times when stress took a toll on my health. Times when finances were strong, but my Faith was shaky. Those seasons taught me how dynamic and ever-developing all these truths about "wealth" are. And that it all demands consistent maintenance. That's why this book doesn't end with a victory lap but with action. Because True Wealth is *lived*, not owned.

In addition to supplementing and supporting the measurement of outcomes, look at the patterns and rhythms of your life. There's nothing wrong with asking, "What did I earn today?" but pair it with asking, "Who did I become today?" Every morning workout, every quiet prayer, every family dinner, every moment of gratitude are the things that matter and grow our real "portfolio." Those are the investments that keep paying dividends long after the numbers fade.

People think success looks like a straight line, but it's closer to a cycle. We build, we falter, we realign. We learn, and make changes, and sometimes even reset. And in that cycle, perseverance matters more than perfection. It's not about getting it right every time, because that's not humanly possible. It's instead about returning to what matters every time we drift.

The Roots of Discipline

When I trace back the habits that anchor me today, they all lead to the lessons I learned as a teenager. Back then, I tried to build a new life after being bullied. I didn't have mentors or money. I didn't have a full understanding, either. But what I did have was pain and a decision to do something with it.

Every day I woke up determined to prove *something*. To others, yes, but mostly to myself. And that became the fuel for my purpose. I trained harder, studied longer, and focused on changing my own story. And what I didn't realize then was that, at the same time, I was building a foundation that would last for decades, and I'm reaping the benefits of that now.

Discipline wasn't about punishment, but direction. And every lesson from those years still shapes how I live today.

1. Consistency Beats Intensity

When I was younger, I thought change came from big, dramatic efforts. I'd go all in, burn out, and start over. But eventually, I learned the power of steady work. Small, consistent effort—applied daily—outlasts any burst of motivation. And that lesson applies to everything now: finances, health, faith, and relationships. Consistency compounds.

2. Pain is a Teacher

The bullying I endured taught me fortitude. It showed me that pain can either break us or build us, depending on how we respond. I carried that with me later in life, so when business or personal challenges came, that same mindset got me through it all.

3. Effort Creates Our Identity

In my youth, I wasn't naturally confident. But every workout, every goal I hit, and every moment I refused to quit were bricks in the wall of who I became. And along the way, I learned that identity isn't something we find, but something we build through repetition.

4. Vision Pulls You Forward

Even as a teenager, I had pictures in my mind of who I wanted to be. And that vision gave my efforts meaning. And it still does. When I see myself walking on that beach at ninety, I know exactly what I'm working toward. Without that vision, all the effort feels endless. But *with* that vision, it feels necessary.

Those same principles I learned then still show up every day now. They're quiet habits that don't make headlines but change lives. Waking up early to move my body before the world gets noisy. Writing down gratitude each morning to center my focus. Checking in with my team and my family before diving into numbers or plans. Turning off my phone at dinner. Reviewing my goals weekly to stay aligned instead of "busy." Spending time in prayer or silence to remember that control isn't the same as peace. These aren't chores, but choices that keep my life aligned with the vision that started all of this.

The teenager who once trained out of pain grew into a man who builds out of purpose. What used to be about proving myself is now about preserving what matters. That's the difference between survival and giving. Survival asks, "How do I protect what's mine?" Giving asks, "How do I grow what's been entrusted to me?"

True Wealth is knowing that every decision affects more than your bank balance. And that change in mentality is what defines a life well-lived.

Returning to the Vision

When I close my eyes and picture that walk on the beach, I can almost *feel* it. The sand under my feet. The whoosh of the waves. The hand in mine. Every pillar stands behind that moment like a quiet guardian, and that vision reminds me daily of what matters most, keeping me from drifting into the chaos and never-ending demands of achievement.

Every pillar in this book leads to one truth: wealth isn't what we have, but how we live. It's how we show up in our bodies, with our families, in our faith, through our service, for our legacy, for our peace, for our awareness, and despite our finances. It has nothing to do with trophies or titles. Instead, it's measured in the moments we live aligned with our values.

But you might be wondering, "How do you balance it all?" My honest answer is, I don't. Balance isn't about equal time. It's about figuring out which priorities take center stage in your daily experience and reordering them. You'll never score a perfect ten across all eight pillars every day. Life doesn't work like that. Some days, you'll be strong in faith but tired in health. Some seasons, you'll give everything to family and let business take the back seat. Other times, the focus will change again. What matters most is noticing which parts of your life need care before they start to crack, and staying aware enough to keep adjusting.

Think of it like surfing. You never stand perfectly still on the board. You're constantly shifting, bending, and recalibrating to stay upright. That's what living in alignment feels like. When you accept that balance demands movement, you stop beating yourself up for being human and realize that what matters isn't how evenly your life is divided, but instead how intentionally your time is invested.

Success comes down to knowing which true elements of wealth need our attention right now, and re-evaluating that list of priorities every day.

Life moves in seasons, and each one demands something different from us. There are seasons to build and seasons to breathe. Seasons to give and seasons to heal. When my firm was new, work dominated my time, which meant the pillar of finance was in the spotlight because it needed to be. Then, when I remarried, family took priority. I learned to slow down, to listen, to rebuild trust and connection. Whenever my health faltered, peace and my Faith became non-negotiable, and I learned to rest without guilt. Each season taught me that priorities change, but alignment remains the constant goal.

And we can't manage what we don't measure. That's why I encourage people to check in with their pillars regularly. Recalibration doesn't require massive life overhauls, but putting time and attention into small, consistent reflection. When we take time to pause and evaluate where our attention is going, we're able to live by design instead of operating on some kind of socially pushed default.

Here's a roadmap you can use to practice that awareness:

The Weekly Check-In

Once a week, sit down with a pen and paper and review the eight pillars. For each, ask yourself two questions: How did I honor this pillar this week? And what does it need from me next week?

You don't need to write paragraphs. A few honest sentences per pillar are enough.

Example:

- Health: Worked out four times but skipped stretching. Need to prioritize recovery.
- Family & Friends: Dinner with the family—felt connected. Call Mom next week.
- Faith: Attended service. Need more quiet prayer time mid-week.
- Peace: Felt anxious on Thursday; too many screens. Unplug earlier.

You aren't grading yourself, but ensuring you remain aware of how you engaged with each of these pillars.

The Thirty-Day Journaling Challenge

If you want a deeper reset, try this challenge: thirty days, eight pillars, four reflections per pillar. That's one reflection per pillar every few days.

Here's how it works:

1. Create eight sections in a notebook or digital journal, one for each pillar.
2. Each day, write about one pillar. Rotate through all eight until you complete four entries per pillar by the end of the month.
3. Use prompts to guide your reflection.

For example:

- Health: What's one habit I'm proud of? What's one small improvement I could make?
- Family & Friends: Who did I connect with meaningfully this week? Who needs to hear from me?
- Faith: When did I feel supported by something greater than myself?
- Service: How did I give time, attention, or kindness to others?
- Legacy: What story about me is being written through today's choices?
- Peace: When did I feel most calm or centered this week? What disrupted it?

- Invisibles: What quiet moments brought me joy or gratitude today?
- Finance: Did my spending reflect my values? Did I plan with purpose or react impulsively?

By the end of the thirty days, you'll start to see patterns, and you'll know where you're doing well and where you're struggling.

The Monthly Reflection

At the end of each month, take an hour to zoom out. Look over your notes from the weekly check-ins or journaling challenge and ask yourself: which pillar feels strongest right now? Which one needs more attention? What small adjustment will help realign me next month?

You don't need to overhaul your life every month. Just choose one focus area and commit to it. Maybe it's reconnecting with family. Maybe it's improving sleep. Maybe it's simplifying your finances. The point is to stay present and engage mindfully.

When you track your pillars regularly, you'll be able to notice changes before they become problems, and recognize signs of imbalance early. Which, in turn, will allow you to respond before burnout hits. Awareness also deepens gratitude. When you write down what's working, you start appreciating the quiet progress you might otherwise miss.

The Two-Pillar Rule

If you can keep just *two* pillars strong, you're doing enough. Or, as I like to say, you can only eat an elephant one bite at a time.

There will be seasons when life demands more than you think you have to give. In those moments, focus on the two pillars that matter most to your survival and sanity. When I was navigating that chaotic season with our new baby, Tehani, those two were family and peace. But during other times, they've been health and finance. It changes, and it *should* change. Two strong pillars can hold you steady until the others catch up. And when life stabilizes again, you can rebuild the rest from a place of strength.

Start small:

- Schedule a fifteen-minute reflection once a week.
- Write one line per pillar instead of a full paragraph.
- Choose one pillar each month to focus on improving.

Over time, those small actions compound. They build awareness, discipline, and gratitude.

We can't pour into every pillar every day. But we can give our best to what matters most right now. And when we stay aware, we know exactly what matters to us during that moment or season. Since there's no such thing as living a perfect life, only a life that's most meaningful to us, focus on being present in your experiences.

Defining Success on Your Terms

You've seen what real wealth looks like in action. But awareness alone isn't enough. If you want to keep living by these principles, you need something tangible that keeps your values front and center.

Traditional vision boards are filled with pictures of vacation homes, dream cars, and travel destinations. They're visual motivation, but too often, they're built around *stuff.* A True Wealth Board is different. It's about how you want to live instead of things you want to own. Unlike traditional vision boards, it's a compass of values. Think of it as your personal reminder of what success means to you, not to anyone else.

How to Make a True Wealth Board

1. Start with a poster board, a corkboard, or a digital canvas.
2. List the pillars. Write them down at the top or around the edges.
3. Add visual anchors. Find images, words, or symbols that represent what each pillar looks like at its best. Here are some examples:

    d. Health: maybe it's a pair of running shoes or a photo of your favorite hiking trail.

    e. Family & Friends: a picture of your kids, or a meal shared with loved ones.

    f. Faith: something that centers you, like a candle or a quote.

    g. Service: an image that reflects generosity or teamwork.

   h. Legacy: something that represents your impact, such as a handwritten note, a family photo, or a project that outlives you.
   i. Peace: maybe a quiet landscape, or a simple phrase that reminds you to breathe.
   j. Invisibles: something symbolic: a wave, a coffee cup, a laugh.
   k. Finance: a statement of vision (focused on "enough" instead of "more").

4. Step 3: Add your statement of vision. Front and center, write your personal declaration.
5. Step 4: Keep it visible. Place it where you'll see it daily, like your office wall, bedroom, or on a digital desktop. I used to laminate mine and keep it in the shower.

If you prefer digital tools, you can create your True Wealth Board online using any visual platform (e.g., Canva, Notion, Trello, or a simple photo collage app). Laminated printables are fantastic for putting in the shower to have as a daily reminder while you prepare for your day. But ultimately, the format doesn't matter. What matters is the intention behind it.

A True Wealth Board works because it keeps our focus on what doesn't fade. It's easy to lose perspective when life gets busy. Emails, deadlines, family schedules—everything competes for our attention. This board acts as a daily reminder of what's constant when everything else isn't. Every image and word on that board represents a decision to live aligned.

Words to Live By

Certain phrases stick with us long after a conversation ends. Sometimes it's a quote. Sometimes it's a single sentence that hits at the right time and reshapes how we think. Throughout this book, I've shared a few of those lines, simple truths that came from experience and mistakes. Here I've reiterated some of my favorites. I encourage picking one that speaks to you most based on where you are today. Write it down. Print it. Save it as your phone wallpaper. Tape it to your mirror. Whatever it takes to keep it visible. Let it guide how you show up this week.

Pick your hard.

Life will always ask something of us. Being healthy is hard. Being unhealthy is hard. Working out is hard. Being unfit is hard. Marriage is hard. Divorce is hard. Choose the hard that leads somewhere worth going.

When the sun comes up, you'd better be running.

Every day gives us another chance to move forward. The world doesn't wait for perfect conditions. Progress belongs to those who start anyway.

Peace is staying anchored through any storm life throws your way.

Calm comes from faith that we'll make it through the chaos without losing ourselves. Give up the need for control to embrace it.

Legacy is what you live, not what you leave.

Our impact isn't measured by what's written on a tombstone. It's in the way people speak our names while we're still alive.

True wealth is lived, not owned.

It's not the cars, houses, or accolades. It's health, love, purpose, and peace, all practiced daily.

Enough is the goal.

When we stop chasing "more," and start defining what is enough for us to live happy, comfortable, and fulfilling lives, we can finally find peace.

Choose one and let it become your reminder this month. Ask yourself, "What would my day look like if I lived by that sentence?" And if you live it consistently, it won't just be a quote but a part of who you are.

When I started writing this book, I wasn't trying to build a brand, or publish a philosophy. I was trying to tell the truth. My truth. I wanted to share the real learnings that came from failing, falling, and rebuilding, which most people miss by pretending to have it all together. And each story, each chapter, and each pillar is a piece of that truth.

I've lived on both sides of the concept of success. And the difference between them was always purely a matter of *perspective.*

There's no single formula for success that fits everyone. We all have different circumstances, histories, and dreams. That's why I didn't write this book as a list of rules, but merely ways to reflect on yourself, your values, and who you want to be in the future. I wrote it as a way to see your life through a wider frame, so you can see wealth as more than money, and uncover how rich your life already is.

The Gift of Reflection

If you take anything from this chapter—or this book—let it be this: reflection is the most powerful financial, emotional, and spiritual investment you'll make.

Take time to pause, to check in, to look at your True Wealth Board, and ask, "Am I living by what I say I value?" Don't wait for a crisis to recalibrate. Make reflection part of your rhythm.

And once you've built your True Wealth Board and chosen your guiding quote, put it into action. Share it with your partner, your kids, or your team. Talk about what each pillar means to you. Ask others what it means to them with the goal of connection. Because the richest lives are built in community, through shared effort, vulnerability, and purpose.

You don't have to be perfect to live richly. You just have to be aware, intentional, and willing to keep showing up. Build your True Wealth Board. Choose your quote. Live your vision. And remember, you don't need more to have enough. You just need meaning to feel full.

When we reach a certain point in life, wealth stops being something we collect and becomes something we contribute. We don't lose it by giving it away; we strengthen it. We become truly wealthy when we help others live richer lives, too.

Real change and development spreads through conversation and example. So, teach what you've learned. Mentor someone who's still in the early chapters of their story. Share your insights with the people in your life, personally and professionally. You don't have to be an expert. You just have to be honest. Tell them about your failures as much as your wins. Tell them what worked and what didn't. That kind of transparency changes people by giving them permission to grow without shame.

Sometimes mentorship looks like an intentional conversation over coffee. Other times it's simply listening without judgment when someone feels lost. Regardless, what you've learned has value beyond your own story. And if each of us took what we've experienced about true wealth and shared it with one other person, we'd start a revolution.

One of the greatest responsibilities—and privileges—of understanding true wealth is teaching it forward. We're bombarded with influencers and entrepreneurs posting highlight reels that make us think that's the full story. We have to show ourselves, and others, the rest. We have to model what balance, gratitude, and integrity look like in real life.

And that starts with small moments, like letting people see you apologize, talking about budgeting and generosity, involving your friends and family in giving back, and celebrating rest and kindness as much as achievement. When other people see you living aligned with your values, they'll learn by example without being preached at or scolded.

Give Yourself Grace

Development isn't linear. As we discussed, you'll have seasons when you live your vision easily, and seasons when you drift far from it. Even to this day, I still struggle to keep all the elements of True Wealth balanced. But that's a part of the process. There will be weeks when your peace feels untouchable, and weeks when everything feels off-balance. You might sometimes slip back into old patterns (such as working too much, worrying too often, or reacting too fast). But when that happens, don't judge yourself.

Grace is a form of wisdom. Give yourself permission to be both a work-in-progress and a person of value at the same time. True Wealth demands that we get better at returning from challenges. So, every time you realign, you grow stronger. And every time you reflect, you move closer to the life you envisioned.

Self-Reflection

Which pillar has been your strongest lately? Which has been most neglected?

Think back over the past few months. Which part of your life feels most aligned right now? Is it your health? Your faith? Your relationships? Then ask yourself, which pillar has you feeling out of sync? Maybe it's your peace (the quiet you've been craving but not giving yourself). Or maybe it's service (the joy of helping that's slipped through the cracks). Awareness is the first step toward recalibration.

Don't criticize. Just notice. Then make one small adjustment this week.

Write your own Statement of Vision.

This is your declaration of the life you're building. Keep it simple and real. Maybe it's "I wake up each morning healthy and surrounded by people I love." Or, "I live with peace, purpose, and enough." I break my vision into sections such as health, family, business, or faith, but there's no wrong way to write it. Start with one concept so you can develop your vision in bite-sized, manageable pieces and build each element of True Wealth into it, piece by piece.

Once you've written it, keep it visible and revisit it monthly. Adjust it as your life evolves.

Who do you want to become, and what does wealth mean to that person?

This is the question that defines the rest of your life. Not, "What do you want to earn?" But, "Who do you want to be while you're earning it?" Imagine yourself five, ten, twenty years from now. What qualities do you admire in that version of yourself? Maybe they're patient, grounded, generous, or calm. Now ask, "What would that person's definition of wealth be?" Is it freedom? Family? Faith? Fulfillment?

Once you can describe that future person, you can start living like them today.

Every act of grace and every time you choose alignment over chasing someone else's approval adds to a greater collective richness.

Our modern age is so obsessed with fast results, the idea of slow, steady change might sound unglamorous. But that's where the magic is. Slow change lasts. It's the small, consistent steps that compound into massive changes. Every time you reflect, mentor, give, or rest, you reinforce your foundation, one mindful decision at a time.

Living True Wealth, Starting Now

This story I've been telling, it's not just mine. It's yours, too. The search for meaning, the struggle for balance, and the desire to live fully belong to all of us. We've all felt the tension between success and fulfillment. This book is a reminder that there's another way that honors every part of who we are; a path that lets us pursue success without losing ourselves in the process.

Live your definition of wealth. Out loud, every day. Don't wait for permission. Don't wait for perfect conditions. Start where you are and with what you have. Give yourself grace, give others wisdom, and give the world your best effort.

True Wealth is about becoming whole. In addition to having financial success, the goal is to become rich in love, rich in time, rich in peace, and rich in purpose. That's the life we're building. That's what it means to discover True Wealth.

The Sunrise Principle

"Teach us to number our days, that we may gain a heart of wisdom."
Psalm 90:12

The seed of the idea of True Wealth began as a question after a coaching conference in 2000. And it surfaced in quiet moments when life looked successful on paper but felt unbalanced in practice. And that question (what is wealth, really?) kept pushing forward until it became the framework that shaped this entire book. Each pillar grew out of lived experience: the wins, failures, losses, and rebuilds, and the desire to create a life that felt full, instead of a life that only looked full from the outside.

True Wealth is built through habits, relationships, beliefs, service, and inner alignment. It isn't found in any one chapter of this book, but in the way each chapter links into the next. Every pillar holds the others up. Strengthen one and your whole life strengthens. Neglect one, and the others start to feel the pressure.

This book began with a single premise: wealth has never been only about money. That message sits at the heart of everything that came after. And the experiences shared here show this again and again.

Health sets the foundation. Family and friends create the emotional framework. Faith grounds decisions. Service widens the view. Legacy expands purpose. Peace protects the mind. The Invisibles bring joy into the ordinary. Finance provides support instead of becoming the center. And all eight pillars work together, not in competition with one another. The more aligned they become, the richer life feels.

The Sunrise Principle brings all of this together. It reminds us that each day starts with a choice. When the sun rises, life begins again and brings a new opportunity to focus on what matters. Remember that parable from the introduction? Every morning in Africa, a gazelle wakes up knowing it must outrun the fastest lion or it'll be eaten. Every morning in Africa, a lion wakes up knowing it must outrun the slowest gazelle or it'll starve. It doesn't matter whether you're the lion or the gazelle. When the sun rises, you better be running!

That image captures discipline, purpose, and action, and it reflects everything these eight pillars teach. Wealth is a practice of daily movement toward a meaningful life.

Each pillar reflects a lesson learned from real moments that shaped the worldview that eventually became this framework.

Health came first for a reason. It was the first place where change became possible. The bullied teenager who watched "Rocky" and decided to run reshaped his future through small choices repeated over time. The early mornings at the gym, the evolution from donuts for breakfast to intentional eating, the discipline of sleep; each habit was a deposit into the future. Health became the foundation that supported everything else.

We can't buy health, and we can't outsource discipline. Those are earned through consistency.

Relationships formed the second pillar because connection determines the quality of daily life. Childhood taught early lessons about conflict, dysfunction, and protection. And those experiences made later relationship-building a conscious effort. Through marriage, divorce, parenting in different decades of life, and friendships that lasted through chaos, the meaning of relational wealth took shape.

No one on their deathbed says they wish they'd worked more. True Wealth in relationships shows up in the way children speak to you when they grow up, the friends who stay, and the evenings built on presence. Family and friends are the real net worth because they shape memories, healing, laughter, and support.

Faith in God became my anchor. It's a belief in something greater that provides steadiness when everything else changes. Adulthood created a personal form of belief that Jesus is my Lord and Savior, shaped through prayer, gratitude, and ownership of mistakes.

Faith becomes a grounding force during career upheavals, financial stress, and personal transitions. It guided decision-making in quiet ways, and offered an anchor during stormy seasons. And it tied into longevity and fulfillment in the same way the centennial studies showed: belief matters for a long life and a peaceful mind.

Service widened the viewpoint. It reminds us that wealth becomes deeper when shared. The stories in this pillar show that giving creates meaning beyond personal success. Service becomes an investment in lives that continue long after our influence fades from view.

Money helps, but time matters. It's the effort that changes people. And sometimes the greatest service is mentorship, listening, or offering guidance when someone feels lost.

Legacy asks a simple question: "What stories do you want told about your life?" And it's created daily in the way we show up. Legacy is whatever remains standing in the hearts and lives of others after our lives end.

One hundred years from now, the cars will be gone. The watches will be gone. Strangers will live in the houses we worked so hard to afford. Legacy asks us to focus on what outlives the material world.

Peace became its own pillar because without it, wealth feels hollow (at best) and anxiety-inducing (at worst). It's the ability to stay calm through stress, and it shows up when we choose not to allow the chaos of the world to overwhelm us. It comes through boundaries, rest, prayer, breathwork, and routines that restore the mind.

Peace allows us to enjoy what we build. Without it, achievements feel rushed and relationships become strained.

The Invisibles became one of the most personal pillars. These are the moments that feel small but define the soul of a life. These can't be measured or purchased; they must be noticed. These moments cost nothing but create meaning that carries far more weight than any financial achievement.

And finally, Finance appears last because it supports everything but defines nothing. My story shows how money shaped early life through frugality, resourcefulness, learning to work at a young age, and later building a career through discipline and risk. But over time, the meaning of money changed. It became a tool for stability, generosity, and choice rather than the source of fulfillment.

Finance is the carriage, not the crown. When money works in alignment with our values, it creates space for the other pillars. When it takes over, everything else weakens.

This book doesn't end with a victory lap, because True Wealth isn't a state you arrive at. It's a daily discipline, and it demands lifelong recalibration. We never graduate from the eight pillars. We continue practicing and reflecting.

And we don't balance every pillar at once. We shift, adjust, and realign as the seasons of our lives change. Sometimes health leads. Sometimes family leads. Sometimes finances demand attention. Sometimes peace becomes the priority. A wealthy life accepts these changes while staying focused on the whole picture.

Hold on to your Statement of Vision. It reminds you that wealth isn't built through grand gestures, but through the habits that make that walk possible. And every pillar supports that day. Strengthen one, and the day feels brighter. Neglect one, and the day feels harder. The Statement of Vision invites us to create our own future picture and build toward it through daily choices.

Ask yourself:

- Which pillar needs attention today?
- Where am I aligned? Where am I drifting?
- Who do I want to become? And what does wealth mean to that person?

In the beginning, I encouraged you to "pick your hard." It becomes a full-circle moment here. Marriage is hard. Divorce is hard. Fitness is hard. Neglect is hard. Purpose is hard. Regret is hard. Every path asks something of us. True Wealth lies in choosing the version of hard that builds a life full of meaning and starting toward that today. Not someday. Not eventually. Not at the end of a long checklist. But today. Through attention, action, and care. It's built every time we choose a walk over a screen, gratitude over frustration, connection over isolation, service over self-preservation, rest over burnout, or perspective over anxiety.

True Wealth was never far away. It was always present in small routines, family dinners, quiet mornings, long conversations, efforts to help others, moments of faith, and decisions to keep going even when life felt uncertain.

The sun is rising again. And like the lion and the gazelle, it's time to run toward the life you're building. A life rich in the eight pillars. That's the wealth that lasts. That's the wealth you've been discovering in these pages. And that's the wealth waiting for you every morning when a new day begins.

About the Author

Entrepreneur and True Wealth Visionary

A man of faith who moves with intention, Bart Zandbergen is a devout believer in the power of True Wealth. Bart lives and leads his life based on eight True Wealth tenets. These pillars have allowed him to cultivate a purpose-driven life that has become fulfilling beyond measure, despite life's inevitable ebbs and flows. Comprised of health, family & friends, faith, service to others, legacy, peace, the invisibles, and finance, Bart's sphere of fulfillment is cultivated through an artful science that unites beyond what the human eye is trained to see.

Investing more than three decades of service in the wealth management space, Bart Zandbergen founded The Zandbergen Group in 2020. Designed as a firm that assists individuals, families, and business owners in achieving wealth that encompasses more than mere monetary means, the Zandbergen Group has risen to prominence for its signature True Wealth approach.

*Disclosures.

To contact Bart:

bart@bartzandbergen.com

www.bartzandbergen.com

www.ingramcontent.com/pod-product-compliance
Lightning Source LLC
LaVergne TN
LVHW010612100826
845148LV00014B/2932

* 9 7 9 8 9 0 1 5 8 3 9 0 6 *